KAREN AMEN'S

—— THE ——

CRUNCH

WITH TEE DOBINSON

THE LATEST, MOST EFFECTIVE WAY TO FLATTEN YOUR STOMACH

CROWN TRADE PAPERBACKS

ACKNOWLEDGMENTS

To my family: Nancy, Louis and my sisters. This project could never have been completed without your support. Thanks for your patience and love, which has carried me through.

To John Roland and John Czygier (John must be a blessed name in my life). I could not have done it without you.

To Siad, my clients, present and former students, who cheered me on and made me believe I could do it.

To Jan Bowmer for her patience and expertise.

Thanks and love to you all.   KA

Thanks also to Sharon Semenza, Pat Fox and Cannons' members.

                                                              TD

Text copyright © Karen Amen 1994
Foreword copyright © Dr Thomas A. Crisp 1994

Published by Carol Southern Books, an imprint of Crown Publishers, Inc.
201 East 50th Street, New York, New York 10022.
Member of the Crown Publishing Group

Random House, Inc. New York, Toronto, London, Sydney, Auckland

Carol Southern Books and colophon are trademarks of Crown Publishers, Inc.

Originally published in Great Britain by Vermilion,
an imprint of Ebury Press in 1994

Manufactured in England.

Library of Congress Cataloging-in -Publication Data
Amen, Karen.
Karen Amen's The crunch: the latest, most effective way to flatten your stomach /
Karen Amen with Tee Dobinson
   p. cm.
   Originally published: London: Vermillion, 1994. With new introd.
   ISBN 0-517-88338-4 (pbk.) : $15.00
   1. Abdominal exercises. I. Dobinson, Tee. II. Title.
GV508.A53   1995   94-3467
613.7'1 – dc20   CIP

ISBN 0-517-88338-4
10 9 8 7 6 5 4 3 2 1

First edition

Edited by Jan Bowmer
Designed by Roger Walker
Photographs by Roberto Rabanne
Additional photographs by Saul De Groen
Illustrations by Siad Crayton

Printed and bound in Great Britain by Clays Ltd, St Ives plc

CREDITS:
Outfits courtesy of Body Force, Everlast and Avia
Trainers courtesy of Avia and Ryka
Exercises demonstrated by Karen Amen, Tee Dobinson,
Jan Bowmer, Carl P., John Roland and Siad Crayton
Cover modelled by Karen Amen (front) and Reed Mahaulic (back)

Contents

One of New York's premier instructors, **Karen Amen** has been training fitness professionals and the general public for over ten years, with many celebrities amongst her personal clients. In regular demand as a presenter at major international and national US fitness events, Karen holds credentials with the American College of Sports Medicine (ACSM), the American Council on Exercise (ACE) and the Aerobics and Fitness Association of America (AFAA) and is actively involved in their instructor certification programmes.

A former gold medallist in the US National Aerobics Championships, Karen operates out of New York City where she also acts as exercise video consultant to CNBC Television. Acclaimed as New York's 'Queen of Crunch', she has been teaching her crunch method successfully for the past two years.

From a rigorous training in physical education and dance, **Tee Dobinson** (Cert. Ed.) became the UK's first AFAA certification specialist. With fitness qualifications from the Aerobics and Fitness Association of America, Lifeworks UK, the Royal Society of Arts and the YMCA, Tee went on to become the Aerobics Co-ordinator at the prestigious London health clubs, Cannons.

Tee now runs her own fitness consultancy, training instructors worldwide, and manages to retain her high profile in the world of fitness by presenting at international fitness conventions; judging at aerobics competitions; various television appearances and magazine and book work.

Foreword

As a sports physician I have more than a passing interest in abdominal and back muscles. Back problems of all sorts are the bane of all athletes, not to mention the vast number of days lost from work due to low-back pain. Many sufferers have weak supporting musculature, which adds considerably to the problem. So I applaud any attempt to improve awareness of the need for good posture and muscular support in the back, and especially the need for strong abdominal muscles, which are often forgotten, but are just as important in protecting the back.

The practice of exercising to tone up the abdomen is not just a matter of cosmetic appearance, important though that is, but it is essential in order to reduce the risk of back trouble in the future. Here then is a new approach which, while remembering the basic principles, provides new hope for all of us. Any exercise has to be enjoyable, otherwise it is quickly forgotten, and this book provides the reader with a lot of fun while giving them the chance to achieve genuine benefits.

There are no magic wands in fitness, weight loss, or muscle toning. Effort is required, plus a balanced programme of sensible eating, correct posture and regular exercise. This can be difficult to achieve for busy people who may lack the necessary incentives and who may give up lengthy and intensive exercise schedules. Hopefully, this book will provide the motivation for many to achieve their goals, and to look better, feel better and at the same time prevent future catastrophes.

Dr Thomas A. Crisp
Sports Physician
TD, B.Sc., MB, BS, Dip. Sports Med.

'I guess I have run the gamut on what I have tried to make my stomach flat ... starving, eating certain types of food, overexercising, applying creams.

However, Karen's crunch programme has not only given me the flat tummy I wanted but, more importantly, it has also greatly improved my overall shape by teaching me how to use my muscles to support my body correctly.

Once you have the technique, it becomes second nature and the improvement happens in a short amount of time.

Quality over quantity is what this crunch programme stresses, and this is a great philosophy for life in general.'

BROOKE SHIELDS
on *The Crunch*

WARNING

If you have a medical condition, or are pregnant, the exercises in this book should not be followed without first consulting your doctor. All guidelines and warnings should be read carefully, and the author and publisher cannot accept responsibility for injuries or damage arising out of a failure to comply with the same.

Introduction

Congratulations! In picking up this book you have taken the first step towards improving your body shape and the way you look and feel. This book focuses on the body's most common problem zone – the stomach – the *bête noire* of almost every man and woman. A flat stomach is a universal dream, one that transcends all cultures. Everyone notices a person with strong, toned stomach muscles from their posture, how they walk and carry themselves, and how great they look in figure-hugging clothes. Such people always stand out in a crowd.

Yet, for the majority of people, a flat stomach all too often remains a frustratingly elusive goal. So what is the answer? The key is regular strengthening and toning exercise that specifically targets the muscles of the stomach and waist. The good news is that we don't need to perform complicated, time-consuming routines. Just a few minutes a day of the *right* kind of exercise can produce the results we want.

There have been a multitude of abdominal programmes in the past, but this book explains why many traditional exercises may not be as effective as you may think. There are so many myths and so much misinformation surrounding this type of training that most of us waste valuable time and effort on inefficient, non-specific exercises that leave us with little real knowledge of proper form or technique. Consequently, not only do we derive few visible results, but we can also put our bodies at risk of injury. This crunch programme shows the *correct* and *safest* way to tone and firm that stomach and waist, focusing on quality of movement.

The exercises in this book are divided into four individual gameplans based on the latest research. Together they form a comprehensive, high-quality and time-effective programme designed to produce maximum results in the shortest amount of time, with your safety in mind.

Whatever your age or fitness level, this programme can work for *you*, and the exercises are equally effective for men and women. It's never too late to start no matter how weak or flabby those muscles have become. You don't need any prior experience of exercise or any special equipment, and all these exercises can be easily performed at home.

THE CRUNCH

What you will need is commitment, consistency and a genuine desire to see results. If you take all these factors on board, we are confident you will be successful in achieving that firm, flat stomach. In addition, your posture will improve, your likelihood of suffering back problems will decrease and you will be able to carry out everyday physical activities with greater ease.

Interested? Then, let's move on and find out more.

CHAPTER 1

What is the Crunch and Why the Phenomenon?

The crunch is an exercise designed to pinpoint and work the muscle groups of the abdomen and waist – collectively known as the abdominals or abs – with a view to shaping and strengthening the midsection of the body. Toning these muscles has many advantages besides enhancing our appearance, since strong abs are vital in maintaining good posture and body alignment, as well as supporting the back.

The stomach and waist region is one of the first areas of the body to show visible signs of ageing and neglect. If not exercised properly and consistently, the abdominals weaken and lose tone, eventually protruding and producing an unsightly bulge. We all agree that a sagging stomach is unattractive but, over an extended period of time, it could also contribute to more serious physical problems, especially in the lower back.

The abdominals interrelate with the muscles of the back to support the whole torso. Together, they form a natural protective girdle which holds the body's major internal organs in place and provides added insulation against wear and tear from the effects of ageing and unhealthy lifestyle habits. An imbalance of strength and flexibility in the abdominal and back regions results in poor posture and body alignment placing a great deal of uneven stress on the lower back and making this area more prone to injury and pain.

According to the American College of Sports Medicine, eighty per cent of us are likely to develop low-back pain at some time in our lives due to improper posture, faulty body mechanics or weak musculature, and our chances of doing so increase with age. Results of studies by health insurance companies in the US based on health claim returns show that

THE CRUNCH

four out of every five people are suffering or have suffered from some kind of back problem – the number one non-terminal health problem. Eighty per cent of these cases have been shown to be related to poor abdominal strength.

So, with the crunch we have an opportunity to address a condition that is widespread and often extremely painful, without recourse to surgery or drugs. Practical application, observation, and in-depth research has proved the crunch to be the most effective and safest way of directly strengthening and toning the midsection of the body.

Just five to fifteen minutes a day of proper crunching, combined with some back stretching and strengthening exercises, is sufficient to achieve the abdominal control we need to maintain proper postural alignment and protect the back against injury. At the same time it will enable the body's natural support system to fulfil its function and delay some of the wear and tear that occurs with the ageing process. And, the added bonus is we will improve our overall body shape, look good and feel great.

So, if you would like to fight the ageing process, acquire excellent posture and reduce your likelihood of back problems while rediscovering a flat stomach, then read on.

IS THE SIT-UP DEAD?

The sit-up has traditionally been one of the most commonly practised methods of strengthening the abdominals. Yet, although the full sit-up may have its place in sports' and athletics' training, not only has it proved to be an ineffective and unspecific way of attempting to change the shape of the abdomen and waist, but it is also potentially harmful to the back.

In recent years research and studies have found that the full sit-up in fact utilizes the abdominals very little in relation to other muscle groups, in particular the hip flexors – the muscles located at the top of the thighs which, together with the quadriceps (the front thigh muscles), are responsible for the bending action at the hips. With a full sit-up the abdominals are responsible only for the first 30-45 degrees of the lift. Thereafter, most of the work is taken over by the hip flexors, consequently minimizing abdominal activity.

The main hip flexor muscle extends from the thigh bone and attaches to the spine at the low-back region. Therefore, each time we lift to perform a full sit-up, this hip flexor exerts a pull from the top of the thigh to the lower back, exaggerating the natural curve of the spine and greatly increasing the risk of injury. If we speed up the movement we multiply that force, significantly enhancing our chances of overstressing the back. In particular, old-style sit-ups with straight legs or double leg raises place a great deal of uneven pressure on the discs (soft tissue) of the spinal column, adding even more stress and discomfort to the lower back region, making it more prone to injury.

Compared with the crunch, therefore, it is clear that the sit-up is a far less efficient way of achieving a flat stomach, providing relatively few direct benefits for the abdominals, yet the risk of injury can be high.

HOW THE CRUNCH HAS REVOLUTIONIZED THE ABDOMINAL WORKOUT

The crunch is a more specific, controlled movement which primarily works the muscles of the stomach and waist, substantially increasing the effectiveness of the exercise while significantly reducing the risk of injury to the back.

Essentially, the crunch is a curling or rounding of the spine which activates the muscles of the stomach and waist area. With the basic crunch position the rib cage comes towards the pelvis, and the lower and middle back remain fully supported by the floor to minimize the work of the hip flexors and isolate the abdominal muscles for a focused, injury-free workout.

There are many variations on the basic crunch movement, and each is designed to target one or more of the abdominal muscle groups that comprise the midsection of the body. Exercising each of these muscle groups according to its major function is essential in developing the strength we need to hold the stomach area flat. Let's take a closer look at the muscles we will be targeting.

Rectus abdominis
This muscle runs down the middle part of the torso – the area we most want to hold flat. Extending from the middle of the rib cage to the pubic region it is one long slender muscle (not two, an upper and a lower, as is commonly thought). We use this muscle when we bend the spine forward, bringing the rib cage and pelvis towards each other, as in a forward or reverse crunch. This action is known as forward flexion.

THE CRUNCH

Internal and external obliques

If we want a narrow, slim waist, then these are the muscles to use. Extending from rib to hip at each side of the body, they are responsible for rotating the torso and also assist in forward flexion. Adding a twist to the basic crunch movement strengthens these muscles, pulling them in and up to give us that neat cinched waist. Each time we exercise one internal oblique we also automatically work the external oblique on the opposite side of the waist.

Transverse abdominis

The many fibres of this muscle spread out across the lower region of the abdomen in a fan-like fashion from the ribs to the pelvis. Peaking in width at the centre and tapering off at each side of the pelvic region, they act as part of that natural girdle for the internal organs. Try taking a deep breath, then exhale – this is the muscle that allows you to force the air out and at the same time hold the lower region of the abdomen flat – an essential technique in all crunch exercises.

The purpose of this book is to help you train these abdominal muscles specifically and efficiently, utilizing them in a way that most closely imitates and enforces their natural action. Once you have mastered the basic crunch technique, you will find that, unlike the sit-up, you won't have to perform excessive numbers of repetitions yet you'll see even better results, without compromising the health of your back. And fewer repetitions means less time spent exercising each day.

The crunch is one of the few forms of exercise that can be done safely by everyone – everyone who wants to look and feel good, have a firmer, flatter abdomen, proper posture and stress-free alignment. You don't need any previous exercise experience. Young and mature, men and women alike can perform this programme and work out at their own level, providing they have no orthopaedic limitations or current injuries.

We have clients in their eighties who, through their solid crunching and back strengthening work, have excellent posture and show no symptoms of back problems. All have firm, well-toned abs and still maintain their cinched waists. Many younger clients have found that regular crunching has helped relieve everyday aches and pains and enabled them to carry out their favourite sports' activities with little or no incidence of injury.

To find out how to make this crunch programme work for you, turn to the next chapter.

CHAPTER 2

Making This Crunch Programme Work For You

This book leads you step by step through four separate gameplans which together form a dynamic, progressive programme, ranging from the most basic crunch techniques in Plan One to the more challenging moves in Plan Four. Here you will find the safest, most effective collection of exercises based on the most up-to-date research. The exercises have been selected for their low risk/high benefit ratio and enable you to achieve and maintain your goal without spending a great deal of time exercising each day.

The crunch is one of the few forms of exercise where the emphasis is on quality of effort and technique rather than quantity. This is one of the reasons we can work the stomach and waist area and effect an improvement in such a short period of time. No matter how many abdominal exercises or repetitions we perform, if we do not apply the proper technique, our results will be poor.

Whether you are a first-time or regular exerciser, this programme can work for you. All we ask for is consistency, and commitment to start you on your way. Consistency is an important factor in any exercise programme and this one is no exception. Whether you work out for five or fifteen minutes a day, staying with this programme will make it easier to see and feel your progress and ensure you obtain results.

HOW TO USE THE GAMEPLANS

Each of the four gameplans is self contained, incorporating a balanced selection of exercises. The aim is to work your way through the plans in a

THE CRUNCH

gradual progression, culminating in the Crunch Challenge in Plan Four. Each plan is carefully designed to build on the strength and knowledge acquired in the preceding plan, so it is essential that you are fully confident with each individual plan before moving on to the next. Think of each exercise as a link in a chain, and each plan as a segment of that chain. You are aiming eventually to link all these components together to form one long chain.

In Plan One we learn the most basic, simplest crunch techniques, focusing on quality of movement by applying the correct positioning and breathing guidelines.

In Plan Two we concentrate on the development of strength as we gradually increase the intensity of the workload to the muscle groups and vary the speed of reaction time, using all aspects of proper form and technique acquired in Plan One.

Plan Three introduces a greater variety and complexity of movements as we vary the speed and positions to 'shock' the muscle groups. Challenging the muscle groups in different ways, for instance by changing the accent or tempo of a movement, is one of the best methods of ensuring progress.

Finally, in Plan Four we face the ultimate Crunch Challenge, fully utilizing all the skills acquired in Plans One to Three with the most demanding combinations of movements and positions.

Most of the concepts introduced in this programme are not widely known. Whatever your fitness level, therefore, it is important that you start with Plan One and stay with that plan until you are completely familiar with the basic techniques. Each successive plan will extend your skills and strength, taking you a stage further towards that ultimate goal, so make sure you master each plan before progressing to the next. Don't rush through the plans thinking you'll see results more quickly. You won't. Remember, the key to your success lies in developing quality of technique and control.

Once you have successfully completed Plan Four, you can then start to interchange the plans as you wish to fit the time you have available on any particular day. In fact, we recommend you do this occasionally to vary the positions and stimulate the different muscles. In addition, for more of a challenge, you can start to use the variations included in Chapter 5 to further increase the intensity and vary the speed or the accent of contraction in the movements. This makes for a truly flexible programme in which you have complete control.

Make these plans work for you in a way that most conveniently fits your lifestyle. If for any reason you stop the programme for a week or so (although you'll feel so good we know you won't want to) then go back to

Plan One and refamiliarize yourself with the basic techniques before you restart the programme.

Warming Up and Cooling Down

All exercise is more effective if you warm up beforehand and cool down afterwards. You wouldn't attempt to play football or any other kind of sport without some kind of warm-up, and the same applies to any exercise programme if it is to be performed well. Start your crunch routine each day by doing the warm-up movements on pages 19–33. Warming up the major muscle groups in this way acts as a rehearsal for the work to follow. Putting the body through a full range of motion will keep the muscles supple to minimize soreness and help prevent injury.

Likewise, at the end of your crunch exercises make sure you cool down properly by following the stretches on pages 92–100. This enables the muscles to relax and allows the body to return to its pre-exercise state.

Back Strengthening

To complement your workout we have included some simple back strengthening exercises on pages 103–108. Performing a few of these directly after your 'crunch' cool-down will help keep the back muscles strong and supple, enhancing the effectiveness of your crunch workout and increasing strength and flexibility in the whole torso. Always finish with the cool-down stretches at the end of the back strengthening section.

How Much Time Do I Need to Spend on the Exercises Each Day?

How much time you spend on the exercises each day depends on your individual ability. Guidelines are given for the number of repetitions, but if you are a complete beginner or have not exercised for some time start with, say, four repetitions of each exercise or as many as you are able to perform in a slow, controlled manner. If you find you are only able to do two repetitions of each exercise at first, then that is also fine. You will still be heading towards your goal of a firm, flat stomach. Remember, it is *your* programme and you should work at the level that is comfortable for *you*.

With abdominal exercises it's usually the neck and shoulder muscles that tire first. As your body becomes stronger and your technique improves the ability to complete more repetitions will occur naturally and you will be able to move through the repetitions in progressively less time.

Compared with other muscle groups, the abdominals take a long time to fatigue and are best worked in what we call 'giant sets'. This means you can perform a greater number of repetitions before you need to rest. Aim to gradually build up the number of repetitions to result in a high-quality, fifteen-minute daily workout.

How Often Will I Need to Practise this Programme?

In order to improve your body shape you will need to practise this crunch programme four or five times a week, or every alternate day. However, if you have completed, say, two days of the programme and are feeling a little sore, on the third day you may wish to take a break and just practise the warm-up and cool-down series of movements on pages 19–33 and 92–100. These will help reduce any soreness as well as maintaining your flexibility and keeping your range of motion constant.

Although the abdominals are one of the few muscle groups that can be worked every day if you choose, we do recommend that you take one day off each week to rest, especially if you are new to exercising.

When Is the Best Time of Day to Do the Crunch Workout?

There is no optimal time of day to perform the crunch workout, as long as you don't exercise straight after a big meal, and you may want to allow at least an hour in between exercising and going to bed. Otherwise, the best time is the time that suits you, whether it's first thing in the morning, during your lunch break or in the evening. Remember, we're only talking about five to fifteen minutes a day.

However, if you know that once your day begins you'll be rushed off your feet and get caught up with numerous other time-consuming activities, plan to do your workout as soon as you get out of bed, before you do anything else. You don't have to perform it at the same time each day, but many people find it helps to have an established routine – just do whatever works for you. The important thing is to make sure you do it!

How Soon Will I See Results?

Your rate of progress will be determined by your quality of movement and your consistency in adhering to this programme. If you follow the programme correctly and consistently for five to fifteen minutes a day,

THE CRUNCH

four or five times a week, you should start to see results within one month and really good results within three. And once you have achieved that ultimate goal of a firm, flat stomach, you will only need to perform your chosen fifteen-minute workout three times a week in order to maintain your fabulous new shape. Should your goals change, you can always adapt your programme or add on an extra day if necessary in order to see further improvements.

We strongly recommend that you keep a record of your progress by completing the training log at the end of this book (see pages 121–122), particularly when first starting out on this programme. Charting your progress in this way will encourage you to be consistent in your efforts to achieve your goal.

What Else Can I Do to Enhance My Results?

In order to obtain results you have to really *want* them and be able to visualize them too. Your mental commitment is just as important as your physical effort. The fact that you are reading this book means that you obviously do want to make some changes to your body shape and health. Picture yourself with a flatter, firmer stomach, and say to yourself, I want to look and feel better, I want to be stronger and healthier, I want to avoid low-back problems. Just try it – it really does work. As you complete each plan, focus on how good and strong you feel, and it won't be long before you see that flat stomach. Visualizing your goals is the first step to achieving them.

Do plan ahead and make some time for yourself. We tend to give so much time to others throughout the course of the day, often neglecting our own needs. Don't you think you deserve some time too? Even if it's as little as five minutes a day, tell yourself this is *your* time, the time you are going to use to make some real changes to your body shape and health.

Applying a little mind preparation throughout the day as well as immediately before your workout will help to make that mental connection and assist in achieving the quality of movement you need. Turn your thoughts inward and really concentrate during your exercise period. Focusing on the benefits you will obtain will enhance your chances of success and enable you to see results more quickly.

Anything Else I Should Know?

As an integral part of this programme, we ask you to make a concerted effort throughout the day to practise good posture habits – when you are

standing, sitting, cooking, washing up or talking on the phone. At all times be aware of how you are actively using your stomach and waist muscles to hold your torso erect to fight the effects of gravity that occur with the ageing process.

While you are working to achieve that fabulously toned stomach, why not take a look at some of your other lifestyle habits? For all-over fitness and optimum health we suggest you supplement this programme with some form of aerobic activity such as walking or swimming, and a sensible, well-balanced eating plan, low in fat and containing plenty of complex carbohydrates.

What You Can Expect From this Crunch Programme

Followed correctly and consistently this programme can:

▶ give you a flat, firm stomach
▶ pull your waist in and improve your overall body shape
▶ make you look good in figure-hugging clothing
▶ benefit your health and make you feel great
▶ enable you to achieve and maintain proper posture and alignment
▶ strengthen the body's natural girdle to provide proper support for the internal organs and the back
▶ improve your breathing technique
▶ significantly reduce your likelihood of suffering low-back problems
▶ allow you to carry out everyday activities more effectively and with greater ease without common risk of injury.

BEFORE YOU BEGIN

Remember, whatever your fitness level you should start on Plan One to familiarize yourself with the basic positioning and breathing techniques. These techniques form an integral part of the programme, and it is essential to learn them if you are to progress. Go through each of the exercises in the order they appear, noting the tips that accompany each photograph. Perform each exercise in a smooth, controlled fashion so that you gain maximum benefit from each repetition while protecting your back.

THE CRUNCH

Neutral Position

An important part of the technique is learning how to keep your pelvis in what we call the neutral position to maintain the natural curve of the spine. This is the optimum balanced position for your torso throughout the course of the day, whether sitting or standing. You may have been told in exercise classes to flatten or press your back into the floor in order to avoid arching the lower back and placing uneven stress on the discs of the spinal column. Yet research shows that excessive flattening of the back can also place unequal pressure on these discs. Excessive flattening of the lower back diminishes its structural strength. It also forces the body into a pelvic tilt which decreases the range of motion in a crunch by removing the last ten degrees of forward flexion. Before commencing the exercises it is therefore important to find your neutral position (see Plan One) and maintain it throughout the whole of your workout, unless otherwise instructed. The objective is to elongate the back without necessarily focusing on removing the lumbar curve of the spine.

Posture

In addition to your crunch workout, making a conscious effort at all times to maintain good posture and alignment is one of the most effective ways of strengthening the abdominal and waist muscles to stabilize the torso and provide proper support for the internal organs and the back. Throughout the day, whether sitting or standing, concentrate on keeping your shoulders back and down and supporting your back by lifting your abdomen in and up. Think of lifting from the top of the head right through the centre of your body.

Standing

When standing, your feet should be approximately hip-distance apart and your weight evenly distributed between both feet, not over to one side as many of us tend to do. The knees are relaxed rather than pressed back in a hyperextended position. The lower back is neither excessively arched forward or backward but in the centre of these two extremes. The abdominal wall is lifted in and up. Shoulders are back and down, completely relaxed. The head, which is a very heavy part of the body, needs to be supported in neutral, resting in the centre of the shoulders and maintaining its natural curve. Don't let the chin jut out but keep the head back just enough to ensure there is no stress on either the front or back of the body. Think of how when holding a new baby we automatically support its head to prevent it from dropping forward or back, yet we often fail to use such care on ourselves.

THE CRUNCH

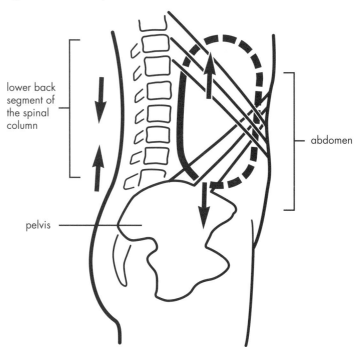

Figure 1: Balanced posture

lower back
segment of
the spinal
column

abdomen

pelvis

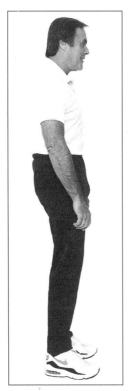

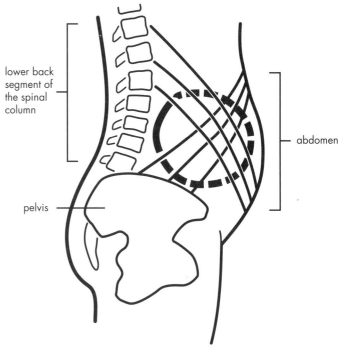

Figure 2: Incorrect posture

lower back
segment of
the spinal
column

abdomen

pelvis

The illustrations opposite show how the abdominal and back muscles interplay to maintain good posture. Figure 1 shows how when the abdomen is pulled in and up, the abdominal cavity is lengthened (indicated by the direction of the arrows), so that there is no uneven pressure on the back. This enables the spine to maintain its natural curve, allowing for greater ease in performing physical tasks without risk of injury.

Figure 2 illustrates how when the abdominal muscles are weak, the abdomen distends and the head and shoulders slump forward to compensate, resulting in increased pressure on the spine (indicated by the lines), which exaggerates its natural curve.

Sitting

If we don't maintain correct posture when sitting (see Figure 3) we place even more stress on the muscles of the back, resulting in uneven pressure on the spine. When sitting, we have a tendency to allow the hips and pelvic region to buckle under, which removes the natural curve of the lower back (see Figure 4). This places just as much stress on this area as allowing the back to arch completely.

Figure 3: Balanced posture   *Figure 4: Incorrect posture*

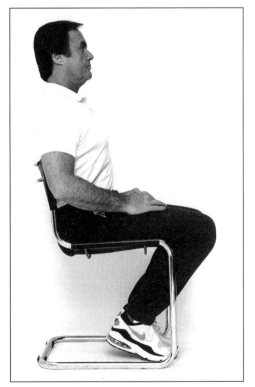
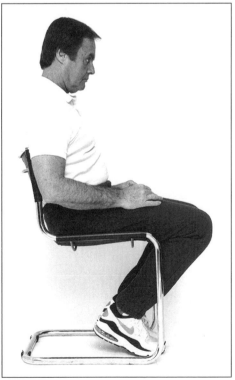

THE CRUNCH

Breathing

We often underestimate the value of proper breathing – one of our most natural assets. In Plan One we will become acquainted with the specific technique to use throughout the crunch programme.

During most activities, our breathing pattern is automatically regulated by the body according to the level of intensity of the particular exercise we are undertaking. Generally, there are no special rules other than trying to breathe smoothly and rhythmically.

However, in the case of strengthening exercises the breathing technique becomes more specific. During the exertion phase of the exercise the air pressure in the chest and abdominal cavity is disproportionately increased. If we do not exhale to release this augmentation in air pressure, discomfort can occur and we are unable to complete the exercise effectively. This can result in an increase in blood pressure – an especially undesirable condition for those who already have elevated blood pressure.

So how does all this affect our crunching? Many people when first starting out have a tendency to hold their breath during the execution of the crunch which causes the abdomen to distend. If we do not breathe out as we raise the shoulders and rib cage, it becomes impossible to compress the abdominals to maintain a flat-stomach position that enables us to complete the exercise successfully.

Exhaling on the lift brings the transverse abdominis muscle into play. As we have seen earlier, the main role of this muscle is forced expiration which allows us to pull the abdomen in and up. Exhaling on the lift therefore allows us to fully involve this muscle to create an decrease in the intra-abdominal pressure. This results in a lengthening of the abdominal cavity and also takes the pressure off the back, important in maintaining good posture (see page 14).

Repetitions

There are many factors which will determine the number of repetitions you are able to complete – your initial fitness level and strength, your mental preparation and whether your body is sufficiently rested, to name a few. Although recommendations are given throughout this programme, there are no hard and fast rules. It is the quality of your completion of each repetition, rather than the quantity, that will give you the best results.

A set generally consists of eight repetitions, performed with *correct* form. *This is only a guideline.* Do not be concerned if you are unable to complete eight repetitions of each exercise at first. Start with the minimum number recommended, initially aiming to gradually build up to one set. Once it becomes easy to complete one set of eight repetitions using correct form, you can start to work up to a second set, adding anywhere between two to twelve repetitions each time you work out. As your muscles become stronger you can then aim to increase the number of repetitions per set to a maximum of sixteen. The golden rule is to progress gradually. Always remember it is more beneficial to add just two more repetitions and perform them well than to attempt twelve more using bad form, for instance by pulling on your neck which we all have a tendency to do when we become tired.

THIS IS YOUR PROGRAMME. YOU MOVE AT YOUR OWN PACE, INCREASING THE INTENSITY AS YOUR ABILITY IMPROVES.

Pregnancy

If you are pregnant, it is important that you consult your doctor before undertaking this or, indeed, any other exercise programme. The Standing Round Over (also known as the standing pelvic tilt) in the warm-up section of this book is a good, safe exercise that most doctors recommend. If necessary it could be performed using a wall for support. Kegel or pelvic floor exercises are also recommended and these can be practised safely before, during and after your pregnancy. See your doctor for further advice. If you are not accustomed to abdominal exercises, then do not attempt any of the exercises in this book.

After the birth, once you have received clearance by your doctor to resume exercising, we recommend that you delay the addition of oblique exercises (exercises which rotate the torso) to your programme until you have given yourself sufficient recovery time.

THE CRUNCH

TEN TIPS FOR CRUNCHING

▶ Always move in a smooth, controlled fashion.

▶ Think of lengthening the lower and middle back towards the floor as you lift to stabilize the pelvis and protect the back.

▶ When starting from the floor, try to lift the full 30-45 degrees. Should you pop up higher than this, the hip flexor muscles come into play.

▶ Exhale as you lift, actively pulling your abdomen and waist in towards your spine and then up towards your rib cage.

▶ Check regularly to make sure your abdominals are not protruding (especially the lower region) by placing your hand on your abdomen.

▶ When supporting your head, avoid clasping or interlocking your fingers behind your neck. Allow your hands to act as a cradle and rest your head in them. This will take the strain off your neck.

▶ Keep your head, neck and shoulders in alignment – in the position that most closely resembles their relationship when you are standing upright.

▶ Avoid looking up at the ceiling during your crunches. Try to look in the direction of the movement.

▶ In exercises where the head is not supported, flex your neck to bring your chin down a fraction as you lift to activate the muscles responsible for supporting the head and neck.

▶ When rotating the torso, lead with the shoulder and keep the elbow back. Before you twist, first use a little forward flexion to bring your rib cage towards your pelvis to ensure that the full range of motion can be completed.

CHAPTER 3

The Crunch Gameplans

Now that you have completed the preliminaries and have a better understanding of how the crunch technique works, let's get started! Remember, whichever plan you are following, always begin your workout with the warm-up and finish with the cool-down stretches.

Warming Up

The purpose of this warm-up is to raise the temperature of the body and muscles and prepare the joints for your workout. Use this time for your mental preparation too by focusing your thoughts and visualizing the results you want to achieve. Your warm-up should leave you mentally and physically ready for the work to follow.

Although guidelines are given, the number of repetitions you do of each movement and how long you hold each stretch for depends on the time of day you take your workout and how stiff you are feeling in any particular session. At first, we suggest you simply move through each exercise to familiarize yourself with the sequence, then start with the minimum number of repetitions recommended.

For preparatory movements to be beneficial they should be performed at a low to moderate speed *without the use of momentum*. Bouncing and rapid uncontrolled movements have no place in this programme. The stretches should be held for a *maximum* of ten counts, since we are not aiming to increase flexibility at this stage – this will happen in the cool-down.

If any part of your body feels especially stiff, you may wish to repeat the warm-up movements for that specific area, particularly if you are doing your workout first thing in the morning when your body is less flexible. Listen to your body and let it be the judge.

WARMING UP

Remember, these movements are just the preparation for your workout, so keep them fluid and easy, avoiding any muscle contraction or tightening.

Start by sitting on the floor. Take a deep breath, then slowly exhale, taking a moment to think about the benefits you will obtain from this programme and how great you will feel once you have begun.

1. Neck Tilts

This relaxes the muscles of the neck. During your crunch workout you will need to take care not to tense your neck or pull on it with your hands.

▶ Sit in a relaxed position with shoulders back and down and your abdomen lifted.

WARMING UP

▶ Allow your ear to gently drop down towards one shoulder, taking care to not to let the shoulder come up – actively press it down.

▶ Repeat to the other side, and continue to slowly move the head from side to side avoiding any fast or jerky movements.

▶ Repeat 8–10 times to each side.

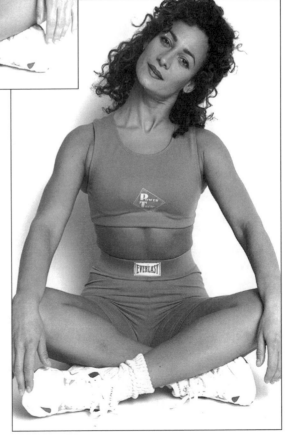

WARMING UP

2. Shoulder Shrugs

This loosens the shoulders, neck and upper back.

▶ Keep the shoulders back and relaxed and feel the lift in your abdomen.

▶ Raise both shoulders towards your ears, then release them down, and repeat. If you wish, as you release, you can roll the shoulders back and down.

▶ Repeat 8–10 times.

WARMING UP

3. Front Shoulder Stretch

This is good for stretching the front of the shoulders, which tend to pull forward as you lift in a crunch. At all times during your crunch workout you will need to keep the shoulders back and relaxed.

▶ Still sitting with your abdomen lifted, interlock your fingers behind your back.

▶ Slide your hands back along the floor, feeling the front of the shoulders and the chest opening up. Hold for 8–10 counts, then release. If you wish, you can increase the stretch by sliding your hands further back.

WARMING UP

4. Seated Round Over

This warms up the muscles of the back.

▶ Sit up tall and raise the arms as shown, keeping the shoulders relaxed and down.

▶ Maintaining that sense of tallness, pull your abdomen in and up as you round over, feeling the stretch in your back. Hold for 8–10 counts, then lift back up to the start position.

5. Forward Lunge

This stretches the front of the thighs (hip flexors, quadriceps) – an important stretch because part of this muscle group connects the thigh bone to the lower back.

▶ Kneel as shown, with hands in line with your front foot. Your chest is lifted and your upper back flat, with shoulders back and down. Your neck is in neutral, maintaining its natural curve. Take care not to let the head drop forward.

▶ Keeping your torso lifted, slowly lunge forward, making sure the front knee remains directly over the ankle. Feel the stretch in the front thigh of the back leg. Hold for 8–10 counts or until you feel the front of your thigh lengthening.

▶ Repeat with the other leg.

WARMING UP

WARMING UP

6. Standing Round Over

This is a good preparatory move for any exercise or sport because it mobilizes and stretches the back.

► Stand, leaning slightly forward from the hips, with knees relaxed and hands on the front of your thighs. Keep your torso lifted and straight.

► Maintaining that lift, round your back, tucking your tummy in. Release, and repeat.

► Repeat 8–10 times, holding the final repetition for 8–10 counts.

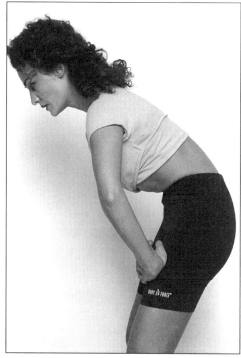

7. Hip Rotations

This mobilizes the hips and the lower back.

▶ Place your hands on your hips and keep your knees bent and relaxed.

▶ In one continuous smooth movement, rotate the hips to the side, to the back, to the other side and return to centre.

▶ Repeat 8–10 times in each direction.

WARMING UP

WARMING UP

8. Trunk Twist

For this movement you will need to use a pole or broom handle. This Trunk Twist warms up the muscles of the waist and also teaches you how to keep the torso stabilized.

Remember, this exercise, along with all the other warm-up movements, should be performed without the use of momentum in order to be effective. To avoid any risk of knee injury it is essential that you follow the instructions correctly. Your abdomen remains pulled in and up, and the area from your pelvis right down to your ankles and feet must remain facing forward, with knees relaxed, throughout this movement.

► Stand as shown with knees slightly bent and shoulders back and down to support the pole. Your abdominals are pulled in and up. Make sure you maintain this lift in the centre of your body and up through the top of your head during the whole of this movement.

▶ Slowly twist at the waist to rotate the torso to one side. Your upper body moves in one smooth unit and your knees and hips remain facing forward to avoid twisting the knees. Return to centre, and repeat to the other side.

▶ Repeat 8–10 times to each side.

Note: *The twist is controlled from your shoulders through to your waist, directly above the rib cage. This is the same area where the twist should occur in all oblique crunch exercises in order to properly train the muscles that define the sides of the waist.*

9. Side Stretch

This stretches the muscles at the side of the waist.

▶ Stand erect with feet a little wider than hip-width apart, knees bent. Place one hand on your thigh to support your body, and reach up with the other arm. Keep the chin in and the shoulders back and down. Try to maintain that lift in your torso without straining.

WARMING UP

▶ Reach over to each side in turn, moving in an easy rhythmic manner. Concentrate on lifting up and over rather than leaning directly to the side.

▶ Repeat 8–10 times to alternate sides. After completing your repetitions hold the stretch for 8–10 counts on each side.

WARMING UP

10. Leg Cross-over

You will feel this stretch first in the hip of your top leg and then in the lower back.

▶ Lie on the floor with legs extended and your body relaxed. Lift one knee in towards your chest and place the opposite hand on the outside of your leg, just above the knee.

▶ Use the hand to bring the leg across your body. At first, keep both shoulders and as much of your back on the floor as is possible and feel the stretch at your hip. Then allow the knee to go further to extend the stretch into your lower back. Hold for 12–16 counts, then release.

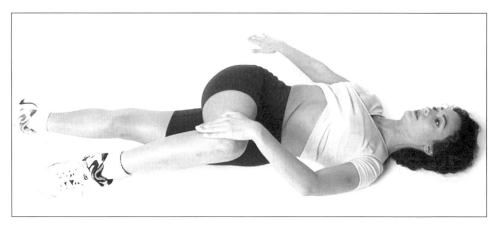

▶ Repeat with the other leg.

WARMING UP

11. Complete Back Stretch

This is good for stretching the whole of the back.

▶ Still lying on your back, clasp your hands under your knees and bring the knees in towards your chest. You should feel a slight stretch in your hamstrings and lower back.

▶ In one smooth action, exhale while lifting your head and shoulders towards the knees to stretch your back. Release, and repeat 8–10 times until your whole body feels loose and relaxed. Hold the final repetition for 8–10 counts.

Remember, if any part of your body felt especially stiff as you were doing these exercises you might want to repeat the warm-up movements for that particular area.

Feeling warm and ready to go?
Then let's move on to the crunch workout.

PLAN ONE: STARTING OUT

Finding Neutral

Breathing Technique

Breathing Crunch

Clean Crunch

Oblique Crunch

Reach Out

Reach Out and Flex

Go For It

Cross-over Crunch

PLAN ONE

Have you warmed up? Then let's start to familiarize ourselves with the basic techniques and positions.

In each photograph note the position of the lower back and the position of the knees in relation to the hips. Most importantly, remember to keep the head and neck in neutral – in the same relationship as if you were standing. This is the optimum position for minimizing stress and fatigue in that area.

Once you have found your neutral position and are confident with your breathing technique move on to the Clean Crunch. In this and the subsequent exercises, try to start with with the minimum number of repetitions recommended. Once you begin to feel a little fatigued, try to do a few more, even if it's just two more. As your technique improves and your muscles strengthen you will be able to gradually increase the number of repetitions. If you are feeling particularly strong you can work at increasing the number of repetitions per set to sixteen where recommended.

Your aim in this plan is to complete two successive sets of between eight and sixteen repetitions with ease and without resting between sets. Remember to move in a smooth, controlled fashion throughout.

> Should you feel any pain or discomfort while performing any exercise, stop immediately. You might want to attempt that exercise again during your next workout session, or when your strength has increased. However, if the pain persists you should consult your doctor.

FINDING NEUTRAL

The following exercise shows how to find your neutral position when lying on the floor. This is the position you should maintain throughout all the crunch exercises unless otherwise instructed.

PLAN ONE

▶ Start by lying your back with knees bent, feet hip-width apart and flat on the floor. Your knees should be placed a comfortable distance from your buttocks. Keep your shoulders relaxed and down. Tilt your pelvis so that your lower back is pressed as far as possible into the floor into a flat-back (pelvic tilt) position.

▶ Now tilt your pelvis away from the floor to create a gap between the floor and your lower back. This is the low-back curve (arched) position.

Finding Neutral continued ▶

PLAN ONE

▶ Gently rock between these two extremes, gradually decreasing the severity of each position until you reach a comfortable, balanced position somewhere between the two. Your abs should be lifted in and up so that your back is lengthening towards the floor but avoiding a complete pelvic tilt.

BREATHING TECHNIQUE

Using the correct breathing technique is essential if you are to complete any crunch effectively. Proper breathing directly affects your ability to hold your abdomen in and up during the lifting stage of the crunch.

Generally, as we inhale the abdomen distends (pops outward) and as we exhale it comes inwards. We need to take advantage of this natural breathing pattern to allow for more control in flattening the stomach area. In the following photographs, take a good look at what is happening to the abdomen.

▶ Lie on the floor and spread your fingers across your abdomen. The middle finger of each hand is pointing towards, but not touching, your belly button. Your shoulders are down and relaxed. Take a deep breath, then exhale. As you exhale, note the direction in which your belly moves.

Breathing Technique continued ▶

▶ Inhale and concentrate on what is happening to your abdomen. Notice how it 'pops' outward.

▶ Now exaggerate both movements so you are able to make a clear distinction between the two. First, exhale and concentrate on using your abdominal muscles to press your abdomen down further. Then inhale, consciously pushing your abdomen out.

▶ Practise this as many times as is necessary until your mind and body begin to make the connection between your breathing and the direction in which your abdomen is moving. During your crunches you will be concentrating on the exhalation phase. The key is to exhale on each lift, each time trying to pull the abdomen further in and up.

PLAN ONE

BREATHING CRUNCH

Let's practise coming up into a crunch using this breathing technique.

Start

▶ Keep your fingers on your abdomen. Take a deep breath and prepare to lift.

Action

▶ Exhale, pulling your abdominals in and up as you slowly round your spine forward to lift your shoulders and rib cage away from the floor. Your mid- and low-back are lengthening towards the floor to stabilize the pelvis and protect the back. Keep your head, neck and shoulders in their natural alignment. Lift only as far as you can while holding your abdomen flat, then return to the start position and repeat.

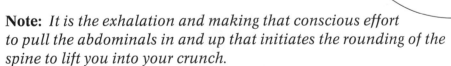

▶ Do as many repetitions as you can until you feel comfortable with this technique.

Note: *It is the exhalation and making that conscious effort to pull the abdominals in and up that initiates the rounding of the spine to lift you into your crunch.*

This technique takes a little practice, so be patient. Once it becomes familiar you will find you automatically breathe out and pull your abdomen in and up as you begin the lift in each repetition of your crunches. When this happens you will no longer need to exaggerate the inhalation phase, and your breath in will be normal and relaxed.

CLEAN CRUNCH

Start

▶ Have feet slightly apart, placed a comfortable distance away from your buttocks so you don't feel any strain on your knees. Cradle your head in your hands. Make sure your pelvis is in the neutral position. Take a deep breath and prepare to lift.

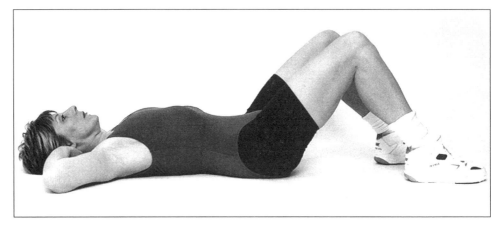

Action

▶ Exhale, pulling your abdomen in and up to lift your shoulders and rib cage off the floor, keeping your shoulders back and relaxed. Your head remains in neutral, cradled by your hands. Only go as far as you can. Keep your abdomen as flat as possible throughout.

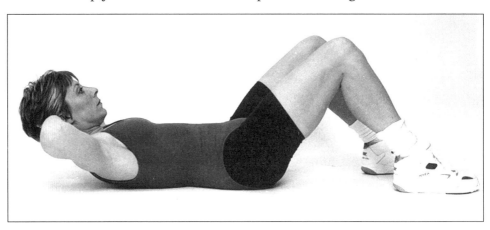

▶ Return to the start position and repeat. Start with 4–8 reps, and gradually work up to two sets of 8–16 reps.

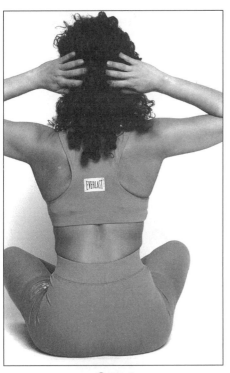

Correct

▶ Note the correct positioning of the hands when supporting your head. Avoid clasping or interlocking your fingers behind your neck, as this will encourage you to pull on your neck. Instead, allow your hands to act as a cradle and rest your head in them.

Incorrect

TRAINING TIPS

▶ Remember, it is the pulling-in-and-up action of the abdominals that initiates the lift. Avoid 'neck-ups', that is when the head and neck take over most of the work causing fatigue in that area. Keeping the neck in neutral should prevent this.

▶ If your stomach starts to protrude during the crunch, stop the movement and make a conscious effort to pull it in and up. If you want to train your stomach to be flat, it is essential that this action is reflected in your crunches.

PLAN ONE

OBLIQUE CRUNCH

Now we're going to start working the obliques – the muscles that give us that narrow, slim waist.

Start

▶ Make sure your pelvis is in neutral. Rock yourself back into position if necessary. Cradle your head with your hands. Imagine your abdomen is sinking into your back and try to maintain this feeling throughout the crunch.

TRAINING TIPS

▶ Make sure you lift first before adding your twist to ensure that the full range of motion is completed.

▶ Lead with the shoulder and rib cage, not the elbow, in order to activate the muscles of the waist.

▶ Remember to exhale on the lift, pulling your abdomen in and up.

▶ Check regularly to make sure your abdomen (especially the lower region) is not protruding. Maintain that pulled-in-and-up feeling throughout.

Action

▶ Start by coming up into a Clean Crunch, then add a twist to the movement by bringing your shoulder and rib cage towards the opposite knee. Keep the elbow back and relaxed to ensure that the twist comes from your waist, not your arm.

▶ Return to the start position and repeat to the other side. Continue alternating sides. Start with 4–8 reps to each side and gradually work up to two sets of 8–16 reps.

REACH OUT

In this exercise one hand is going to support your head while the other hand acts as your lead.

Start

▶ Have one arm raised and aiming beyond your knees. The opposite hand is in the cradle position. Check that your pelvis is in neutral.

All movements should be performed smoothly and with control.

TRAINING TIPS

▶ As you perform the crunch, have your eyes focus over the top of your raised hand so that your upper torso, from your waistband to the top of your head, lifts as one unit.

▶ During the lift take care not to pull the pelvis into a flat-back position. Maintain neutral throughout. Feel your abdominals compressing and your back lengthening towards the floor.

Action

▶ Exhale and use the abdominals to lift you into the crunch, reaching the raised arm towards or past your knees. Keep the arm straight and your head in neutral.

▶ Return to the start position and repeat. Start with 4 reps, building up to two sets of 8–16 reps.

▶ Repeat, raising the other arm. Make sure you do an equal number of repetitions on each side.

PLAN ONE

REACH OUT AND FLEX

Start

▶ Start as in the previous exercise with one arm reaching out in front. Take a few deep breaths, concentrating on exhaling and flattening your abs to reinforce your breathing technique. Let the centre of your torso sink down towards your back and then up towards your rib cage to give you that flat-stomach sensation.

TRAINING TIPS

▶ Remember to exhale as you lift into the crunch, and really concentrate on holding your stomach flat – just think of that ultimate goal.

▶ Keep your head in neutral throughout the exercise. Try not to let it bob back and forth.

Action

▶ This time, as you lift, bring the knee in towards your chest while reaching out with the arm. Think of your pubic bone coming towards your chest along with the knee.

▶ Return to the start position and repeat. Try 4 reps at first and work up to two sets of 8.

▶ Repeat with the other arm and knee, making sure you do the same number of repetitions on each side, with equal concentration on proper form.

PLAN ONE

GO FOR IT

Now you are going to attempt your first crunch without head support throughout. This time as you lift you will need to bring your chin down just a fraction to enable the neck muscles to support the weight of your head.

Start

▶ Start by having your hands cradle your head. Take a deep breath as you prepare to lift.

Action

▶ As you lift, bring your chin down slightly to support the head while releasing your arms and reaching up past the knees. Visualize that tight stomach and waist as you reach.

▶ Return to the start position and repeat. Try to do 4 reps at first, then work up to two sets of 8.

Note: *It may take a little time for your neck muscles to strengthen sufficiently to support the head in this position, so don't worry if you are not able to complete a great number of repetitions at first. If necessary, start with just 2 reps, increasing to 4 the next time you work out. Before you know it, you'll be up to two sets of 8 in no time.*

TRAINING TIP

▶ If at first you find this exercise too uncomfortable without head support, come up into the crunch and release the hands for just a moment, then replace them as you roll back down to the floor.

PLAN ONE

CROSS-OVER CRUNCH

Start

▶ Raise one leg and place the ankle over the opposite knee. Support your head with one hand and place the other hand on your abdomen. Pull your abs in towards your back, using your hand as a guide.

TRAINING TIP

▶ When rotating the torso it is important to keep the elbow back and relaxed. Swinging the elbow forward does not allow the full range of motion to be completed and tends to make you pull on the neck. The rotation should start at the waist, so that the whole of the upper torso moves as a unit.

Action

▶ Breathe out smoothly as you come up, then add a twist to the movement by lifting and rotating the shoulder and rib cage towards the raised knee. Remember to keep the elbow back and relaxed.

▶ Return to the start position and repeat. Start with 4–8 reps, working up to two sets of 8–16 reps.

▶ Repeat to the other side, doing an equal number of repetitions to each side.

Now you have completed your crunch workout for today,
turn to page 92 for the cool-down exercises.

PLAN TWO

PLAN TWO: GETTING STRONGER

Reverse Crunch

Get A Leg Up

Get A Leg Up With A Twist

Garden Fence

Tuck Crunch

Twister

Thigh Slide

Butterfly Crunch

Toe Curl Crunch

Out and Around

PLAN TWO

Have you warmed up? If so, let's get moving with Plan Two. Do not attempt this plan until you feel really competent with the basic positions and techniques in Plan One. We will be using all of these skills to develop your strength in this more challenging sequence of variations. Taking time to progress gradually will minimize any soreness you might feel and also give your body time to adapt to the changes and the new demands being made upon it.

Remember, your target is to complete two successive sets of between eight and sixteen repetitions with ease.

Make sure you apply the correct breathing technique and neutral position throughout the following exercises. If you need to refresh your memory, go back to Plan One and review your basics.

PLAN TWO

REVERSE CRUNCH

As the name suggests, with this crunch we reverse the action so that the movement starts from the base of the spine, bringing the pelvis towards the rib cage.

Start

▶ Start with knees bent in towards your chest as much as possible, lower legs resting on the back of your thighs, ankles crossed. Your legs should feel completely relaxed. Your arms are by your sides, with palms facing upward so that you are not tempted to push with your hands as you perform this crunch.

Action

▶ Exhaling and pressing your abdomen in and up, start to slowly curl the lower part of the spine so that the pelvis moves towards the rib cage. Take care not to pull the knees in to assist, let the abdominals do the work. Your knees will automatically move further in towards your body as your spine curls up from your tailbone.

▶ Return to the start position and repeat. Start with 4–8 reps, working up to two sets of 8–16 reps.

TRAINING TIPS

▶ When in the start position make sure your knees are as close to your chest as possible so that you concentrate on curling the spine rather than on pulling the legs back and forth.

▶ To achieve the best training results, the movement needs to be smooth and controlled. This will prevent you from jerking the lower body up and negating the effect of the exercise.

PLAN TWO

GET A LEG UP

Start

▶ Raise one leg and extend it fully, ensuring the knees are side by side. Cradle your head in your hands and maintain the neck in neutral.

TRAINING TIPS

▶ Be careful not to pull the pelvis into a flat-back position as you perform the crunch. Keep your back lengthened towards the floor and your abdomen compressed.

▶ As you lift, think of the rectus abdominis (the long muscle that forms the middle section of the abdominals) pulling in and up, away from the extended leg.

Make sure you do an equal number of repetitions with each leg.

Action

▶ As you exhale during the lift, pulling the abdomen in and up, try to extend the raised leg even further. Your abdominals are pulling in and up towards your chest and away from the extended leg. Keep the elbows back and relaxed.

▶ Return to the start position and repeat. Try 4–8 reps at first and build up from there. Gradually work up to two sets of 8–16 reps.

▶ Repeat with the other leg raised.

PLAN TWO

GET A LEG UP WITH A TWIST

Start

▶ Start as in the previous exercise with hands cradling the head and one leg extended. Make sure your pelvis is in neutral.

Action

▶ Pull your abs in and up to initiate the lift, then add a twist by raising the opposite shoulder towards the extended leg.

▶ Return to the start position and repeat. Start with 4–8 reps and work up to two sets of 8–16 reps.

▶ Repeat with the other leg extended. Remember to do an equal number of repetitions with each leg.

TRAINING TIPS

▶ Before you twist remember to first use a little forward flexion to bring your rib cage towards your pelvis and ensure that the full range of motion can be completed.

▶ Keep both hips firmly on the floor throughout the exercise.

PLAN TWO

GARDEN FENCE

Start

▶ Cross your arms, placing your hands on the front of your shoulders, elbows aiming upward. Let your chin rest on your arms at the point where they cross. Check that your pelvis is in the neutral position. Feel your abdomen sink into your back as you prepare to exhale.

TRAINING TIP

▶ As you lift up, your chin remains resting in the same position on your arms. It's as if you were leaning on a garden fence for a chat.

Action

▶ Let your breath out smoothly as you lift. Your elbows follow the direction of your thighs and your chin remains resting on your arms. Keep the shoulders down and relaxed.

▶ Return to the start position and repeat. As your head remains unsupported throughout, start with just 4 reps and gradually work up to two sets of 8-16 reps.

Throughout the exercises, don't just perform the movements, but visualize them too. Focus your thoughts and picture your stomach flattening – if you can't perceive it, how can you expect to achieve it?

TUCK CRUNCH

This exercise combines the actions of the Clean Crunch and Reverse Crunch.

Start

▶ Have your knees as close to your chest as possible, and cross your ankles. Your legs are completely relaxed, and your hands are cradling your head. Pressing your abs in towards your back, take a deep breath and prepare to exhale.

Action

▶ As you lift, curl the spine up to bring your rib cage and pelvis towards each other. Avoid pulling up quickly or relying on momentum to achieve your tuck. Keep the movement slow and controlled.

▶ Return to the start position and repeat. Start with 4–8 reps, building up to two sets of 8–16 reps.

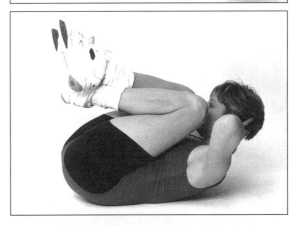

PLAN TWO

TRAINING TIP

▶ Remember, it is the tightening and flattening action of the abs that brings the rib cage and pelvis towards each other. Keep this in mind as you perform the crunch. Imagine your navel is disappearing into your middle.

TWISTER

There's plenty to think about as you perform this crunch, so take your time at first and move slowly through each position. The more familiar the exercise becomes, the less time it will take to complete. However, always ensure you use proper form throughout to maximize the quality of your crunches.

Start

▶ Start in the same position as the Tuck Crunch. Your legs and knees are completely relaxed and your hands are cradling your head.

Action

▶ Use the abdominals to lift you, then add a twist, reaching one arm past the outside of the opposite leg. At the same time the hip of this leg is aiming towards the armpit of the arm supporting your head so that your feet move closer to the raised hand.

TRAINING TIP

▶ Avoid jerking the body up. The whole action should be performed in one fluid movement.

▶ Return to the start position and repeat. Start with 4 reps and work up to at least two sets of 8.

▶ Repeat to the other side, making sure you do an equal number of repetitions to each side.

Don't forget your breathing technique.

THIGH SLIDE

PLAN TWO

Start

▶ Rest your hands on the front of your thighs. Bring the chin down just a fraction to support your head, but make sure you can keep the neck relatively in line with the spine.

Action

▶ As you use your abdominals to lift you into the crunch, slide your hands forward towards your knees. Lift your rib cage as high as you can while maintaining that flat-stomach position.

▶ Return to the start position and repeat. Start with 4–8 reps, working up to two sets of 8–16 reps.

TRAINING TIPS

▶ As you lift, have your eyes focus over the top of your hands or your knees.

▶ If you wish, you can take hold of your legs at the top of the crunch and hold your body up with your arms while you concentrate on holding your abdomen flat.

Note: *At first, if your abdominals start to protrude as you perform this crunch, return to the floor and don't come up so far next time. Instead, concentrate on maintaining control in a smaller range of motion. As you become stronger you will be able to lift higher while keeping your abdomen flat.*

PLAN TWO

BUTTERFLY CRUNCH

Start

▶ Lie with your knees relaxed out to the sides. Place your heels together and keep your ankles in line with the lower legs. Your head is in the neutral position, cradled by your hands. Press your abdomen into your back and prepare to lift.

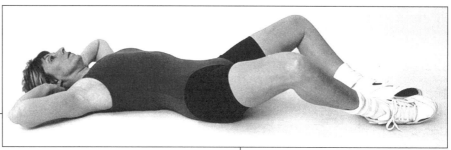

Action

▶ As you lift into your crunch, really concentrate on flattening your abdomen, pulling in and up from the pubic region to the rib cage. Make sure your pelvis remains in the neutral position.

▶ Return to the start position and repeat. Try 4–8 reps to start with, and gradually build up to two sets of 8–16 reps.

Note: *If you don't have sufficient flexibility in your inner thighs, having the legs in this open position may cause you some discomfort. Should this occur, each time you complete the exercise, relax the upper body but keep your legs in position for a short while to improve the stretch in your inner thighs.*

TRAINING TIP

▶ Since your knees are not aimed in the direction of the crunch in this exercise, you may find the curve in your lower back is increased. Try to balance this by really concentrating on holding your abdomen in and up, feeling your abs and back elongating towards the floor.

PLAN TWO

TOE CURL CRUNCH

The action in this exercise is similar to that in the Clean Crunch, but as you come up into the crunch you are also going to involve the calf muscles by lifting your heels.

Start

▶ Lie in the Clean Crunch start position with hands cradling your head. Pull your belly button in towards your spine and then up towards your rib cage as you prepare to lift.

Action

▶ As you come up, reach your arms past the top of your knees and lift your heels as much as possible, feeling a strong contraction in your calves. The challenge here is to keep the hips in the neutral position. You can do it!

▶ Return to the start position and repeat. Start with just 4 reps and gradually build up to two sets of 8–16 reps.

Note: *Should you experience a cramping in your calves as you perform the exercise, bring the heels back to the floor and lift your toes towards the ceiling to release the calf muscles. At first, to strengthen your calves, you may wish to just practise the heel lifts without the crunch.*

TRAINING TIP

▶ Avoid placing your weight on your toes as you lift. Keep your weight distributed throughout your torso.

PLAN TWO

OUT AND AROUND

In this exercise you will need to place your feet against a wall.

Start

▶ Have your feet flat against the wall to support your legs. Place one hand on the opposite shoulder. The other arm is straight and aiming towards the top of the knees.

Action

▶ Lift straight up first then twist at the waist reaching the extended arm towards the outside of the opposite knee.

PLAN TWO

▶ Return to the start position and repeat. Start with a minimum of 8 reps if you can, and gradually build up to two sets of 8–16 reps.

▶ Reverse the position of the arms and repeat to the other side. Do an equal number of repetitions to each side.

Note: *Look carefully at the photographs and note the position of the knees in relation to the feet and hips so that the body is is a lengthened position.*

Remember to keep your pelvis in neutral throughout. Re-rock it into position if necessary.

TRAINING TIP

▶ Make sure your twist comes from the shoulder and that side of the rib cage by aiming the shoulder up and around towards the opposite knee. Maintain your neck in neutral by moving your head and upper body in one unit and looking in the direction of the exercise.

Now turn to page 92 for your cool-down exercises.

PLAN THREE: GOING FURTHER

Seated Reverse Crunch

Air Bike

Full Extension

Single Arm Over

Twin Peaks

Head Cradle

Long Crunch

Longest Crunch

Mummy Crunch

Clasp Crunch

PLAN THREE

Well done! Through your careful and skilful application to the crunching techniques you have now progressed to Plan Three. Be proud of your accomplishments.

At this point you should be able to find and maintain the neutral positions for your lower back (pelvis), head and neck with comfort and ease. Your breathing should be consistent during your crunching as you remember always to exhale on the lift. That pulling-in-and-up action of the abs should now be second nature to you – not just when exercising, but also throughout the day, whether sitting or standing. Look in the mirror and see the improvement in your posture.

Now that you have built up sufficient strength, we are going to introduce further challenges in a greater variety of moves to ensure you maintain the progress you have already achieved.

It is essential that you hold the correct positioning throughout each repetition. If, for instance, you find yourself having difficulty holding neutral or your head starts to come forward, or if when performing an oblique crunch your elbow takes over from your shoulder – these are signs of fatigue. If any of these happen, take a break – you have earned it!

Begin with four to eight repetitions of each crunch, eventually progressing to two sets of between eight and sixteen repetitions, performed with ease and without resting between sets. If you are feeling particularly strong and ambitious you might wish to complete more repetitions of your favourite crunches.

Make sure you warm up before you start.

PLAN THREE

SEATED REVERSE CRUNCH

Start

▶ Sit up *very* tall with arms outstretched in front, hands clasped loosely. As with a crunch on the floor, you begin this exercise by pulling the abdominals in and up. Really feel that lift in your body. Imagine your head is being pulled up to the ceiling and your spine is following through.

Action

▶ Maintaining that lift in your middle, exhale and slowly round your spine to bring your pelvis under. As you round the spine further, your torso moves back. You don't want to move too far back at first or you won't be able to hold your abdomen flat. Familiarize yourself with the key points of the exercise first.

▶ Return to the start position and repeat. Start with 4–8 reps and work up to two sets of 8–16 reps.

TRAINING TIP

▶ Avoid that sinking sensation by keeping the abdominals lifted throughout. It is the rounding of the spine that allows you to move back, rather than rocking back and forth at the hip flexors (top of the thighs). Concentrate on developing the proper technique.

PLAN THREE

AIR BIKE

This is a safe adaptation of that cycling exercise we all remember from PE sessions at school.

Start

▶ Raise your legs and bend the knees towards your torso, just enough so as not to feel any strain or discomfort in the lower back, but keep your hips on the floor. Cradle your head with your hands.

Action

▶ Start with a Clean Crunch, then twist at the waist to bring one shoulder towards the opposite knee. As you bring the shoulder up, the knee moves down to meet it. Keep the elbow back and relaxed.

PLAN THREE

TRAINING TIPS

▶ Keep your abs down throughout the exercise. Avoid rocking back and forth and allowing momentum to take over.

▶ Keep your knees above your hips, and make sure your hips and lower back remain on the floor as you execute each twist.

▶ Repeat to the other side and continue alternating sides, keeping the movement fluid. You remain up for the duration of your repetitions. Start with 4–8 reps to each side and work up to two sets of 8–16 reps.

Remember to exhale on each lift.

PLAN THREE

FULL EXTENSION

Start

▶ Start with legs raised and knees bent towards your torso. If you feel any discomfort or strain in the lower back you may bend the knees further, but make sure your hips and lower back remain on the floor. Cradle your head with your hands.

Action

▶ Exhale as you lift, extending both arms towards your feet while straightening the knees and aiming the feet towards the ceiling.

TRAINING TIPS

▶ As you perform the exercise, think of the crunch coming from each end of the long abdominal muscle – from both the pubic region and the rib cage.

▶ Make sure you release the knees towards your torso each time you return to the start position.

▶ Return to the start position and repeat. Start with 4–8 reps, gradually progressing to two sets of 8–16 reps.

SINGLE ARM OVER

Start

▶ Raise one leg, keeping the knee bent. The other foot remains flat on the floor. Your hands are in the cradle position supporting your head. The raised foot is going to act as your guide.

PLAN THREE

Action

▶ Start with a Clean Crunch, then add a twist, leading with the shoulder. As you twist, extend the opposite arm towards the outside of the raised foot. Reach as far as you can, but remember the movement is still initiated by the pulling-in-and-up of the abs.

▶ Return to the start position and repeat. Start with 8 reps and gradually work up to two sets of 8–16 reps.

▶ Repeat with the other leg. Do an equal number of repetitions on each side.

TRAINING TIPS

▶ Keep the raised leg above the hips, with the knee slightly relaxed.

▶ As your arm extends around the leg, towards the raised foot, your arm, shoulder and rib cage move in one smooth unit.

PLAN THREE

TWIN PEAKS

Start

▶ Place your hands in the centre of your back so that your palms are reaching towards your shoulder blades and your arms create a basket to support your head. Extend one leg fully and have it just off the floor, reaching out and away from the body.

TRAINING TIPS

▶ Think of all the energy flowing through the leg as you concentrate on lengthening and stretching it away from the body.

▶ You may be tempted to pull your elbows forward as you lift. Avoid this by making a conscious effort to keep your elbows relaxed. This helps ease any strain on the neck.

Action

▶ As you exhale, pulling your abs in and up, your head, arms and rib cage raise in one unit while your extended leg lifts up smoothly, still reaching out and away.

▶ Return to the start position and repeat. Try 4–8 reps at first, and gradually progress to two sets of 8–16 reps.

▶ Repeat, raising the other leg, making sure you do an equal number of repetitions on each side.

Remember to check that your pelvis is in the neutral position.

HEAD CRADLE

PLAN THREE

Start

▶ One hand is behind your head, with the elbow straight out to the side. The other hand is reaching down towards the shoulder blade, as in the previous exercise, and the opposite leg is extended fully, reaching out and away from the body.

> *Remember to do an equal number of repetitions on each side. Don't forget your breathing technique.*

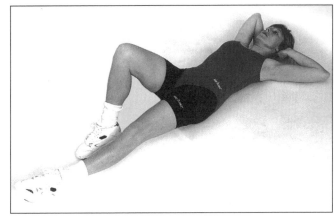

Action

▶ Start with a Clean Crunch and add a twist, bringing the opposite shoulder towards the extended leg. At the same time, lift the extended leg just a little way off the floor, still reaching the leg out and away.

▶ Return to the start position and repeat. Try 8 reps at first, and work up to two sets of 8–16 reps.

▶ Repeat on the other side.

TRAINING TIP

▶ Try not to focus on lifting the leg. Instead, think of lengthening it, keeping the lift small.

PLAN THREE

THE LONG CRUNCH

Start

▶ One leg is raised, so that both knees are touching. Both arms are extended behind your head and placed close by your ears in order to support your head. Your hands are crossed at the wrists. Keep the shoulders relaxed.

Don't forget to do an equal number of repetitions with each leg.

TRAINING TIP

▶ As you lift the upper body, the extended leg does not move. Try to concentrate on lengthening the leg as it reaches out and away from you.

Action

▶ Exhale strongly as you lift your upper body in one smooth unit, reaching out with the extended leg. Having the body in this lengthened position should help you keep your abdomen flat and long for the duration of the repetitions.

▶ Return to the start position and repeat. As this is one of the most difficult working positions for the abdominals, start with just 4 reps, and progress slowly to two sets of 8–12 reps.

▶ Repeat, raising the other leg.

PLAN THREE

THE LONGEST CRUNCH

In this exercise you will need to place your feet against a wall for support. This will allow you maintain your pelvis in neutral while having your body in a lengthened position.

Start

▶ The soles of your feet are placed firmly against the wall and your knees at a comfortable distance from your body. Your arms are extended behind your head, hands crossed at the wrists and fingers extended. Keep your arms close by your ears to support your head. Pull your abdomen flat and prepare to exhale.

▶ Lift your head, arms and rib cage in one smooth movement.

▶ Return to the start position and repeat. Start with 4 reps, and gradually work up to two sets of 8–16 reps.

TRAINING TIPS

▶ Take advantage of this lengthened position to really pull those abs in and up, at the same time thinking long and flat.

▶ Try not to let your shoulders creep up as you lift. Keep them down so that your neck remains long and there is no added pressure on the neck muscles.

MUMMY CRUNCH

In this exercise you start in the up position and remain up for 3 counts. This will greatly increase the level of intensity at which you are working. You might want to start by going through this series of movements 4 times and then build up your number of repetitions from there.

TRAINING TIPS

► Make sure you don't start to roll your body back down to the floor until your hands are firmly replaced on your shoulders.

► When you first start to learn this series, go through each stage slowly, holding in each position and checking that your abs are pulled in and up.

Start

► Your arms are crossed with hands resting on your shoulders. Both legs are raised towards your torso, with knees bent so that you don't feel any strain or tension in the lower back. Breathing out, press the abdominals in towards your spine as you lift up, aiming your elbows towards your knees.

Action

▶ From the up position, extend your arms up past your knees and try to reach up higher while holding your abdomen flat.

▶ As you bring the arms back down to rest your hands on your shoulders, keep the body lifted by continuing to press your abdomen in and up.

▶ After placing your hands back on your shoulders, let your body roll down to the floor.

▶ Take a breather and prepare for your next repetition. Start with 4 reps of this whole series, working up to two sets of 8–12 reps.

PLAN THREE

CLASP CRUNCH

Start

▶ Your feet remain up against the wall to support your pelvis in neutral. Your arms are extended in front, with hands clasped, and directed towards the top of your knees.

TRAINING TIP

▶ As you get stronger, your imaginary partner becomes stronger too, helping to pull you up further.

Action

▶ As you come up into the crunch, imagine someone is standing over you and taking hold of your hands to help you lift up. While they are assisting you to lift, you can concentrate on keeping your abdomen flat.

▶ Return to the start position and repeat. Start with 4 reps, and work up to two sets of 8–16 reps.

Have you maintained your neutral position throughout?

Now turn to page 92 and do your cool-down exercises.

PLAN FOUR

PLAN FOUR: THE CRUNCH CHALLENGE

Boxer Crunch

Oblique Punch Crunch

Follow the Thighs

Crunch on the Bias

Elevated Obliques

Tough Crunch

Double Reach

Climbing Crunch

Killer Crunch

Karen's Crunch

Couple Crunch

PLAN FOUR

Yes, you have made it to the Crunch Challenge!

You should be delighted with your progress so far. Your middle is now stronger, you are maintaining good posture when sitting or standing, and you are looking and feeling fantastic. Well done!

You have mastered the breathing technique and are now able to find and maintain your neutral position with relative ease. As we have stressed throughout this programme, the quality of your crunching is the key to obtaining maximum results without having to spend an excessive amount of time exercising. In this plan the basic rules of proper crunching still apply. Many of the exercises are quite challenging, and you will need to utilize all the skills you have acquired in Plans One to Three. In Plan Four you should not allow even just one repetition to be completed without holding your abdomen flat throughout.

Here, we will be introducing some more demanding positions and combinations of movements such as Crunch on the Bias. Pay particular attention to your body positioning in this exercise, as it is quite different from any of the positions in the preceding plans. Performed correctly, this exercise will firm the sides of your abdomen where the rectus abdominis meets the obliques.

We have included an optional exercise at the end of this plan – the Couple Crunch – which involves working out with a partner. It is not an integral part of the programme, but we hope it will provide an added incentive to your workout.

When first starting any new sequence, always begin with the minimum number of repetitions recommended and aim to perfect your technique. As your strength increases, you can gradually add more repetitions. Remember, each plan is a progression in itself. Your ultimate aim in this plan is to go through each exercise in succession, performing two sets of repetitions without any rest stops. You can do it!

As soon as you have done your warm-up, it's time to meet the Crunch Challenge. Let's go!

BOXER CRUNCH

PLAN FOUR

Start

▶ Have your heels resting comfortably on a chair to support your pelvis in neutral. Your hands are cradling your head.

Action

▶ As you lift, bring your arms up in front to complete a pec (chest) press. Your arms are bent at the elbows with hands in loose fists. As you press the elbows towards one another, squeezing the arms together, keep your shoulders down and your chest lifted.

▶ Return to the start position and repeat. Try 4 reps to start with, then gradually build up to two sets of 8–12 reps.

TRAINING TIP

▶ Aim to hit the maximum range of motion in your crunch and your pec press. Make sure you exhale and press your abdomen down as you lift.

PLAN FOUR

OBLIQUE PUNCH CRUNCH

In this exercise you start the crunch from the up position and only return to the floor when you have completed your desired number of repetitions. This boosts the intensity of the exercise, so do take care and use your judgement as to how long you stay up off the floor. The objective is to keep your abdomen flat throughout.

TRAINING TIP

▶ After reaching across the body, make sure your abs remain flat as you come back to the start position.

Start

▶ One heel remains resting on the chair, the other leg is raised off the chair. The opposite shoulder is lifted towards the raised leg, with the arm bent and hand in a loose fist. The other hand is supporting your head.

> *Do an equal number of repetitions on each side. Don't forget your breathing technique.*

Action

▶ As you lift, extend the opposite arm towards the raised leg while lowering the leg to the chair. Reach across as far as you can, feeling your abdomen lengthen as you bring the leg down.

▶ Return to the start position and repeat. Start with 4 reps and progress gradually to two sets of 8–12 reps.

▶ Return to the floor and lift into the start position to repeat on the other side.

PLAN FOUR

FOLLOW THE THIGHS

Start

▶ Have both heels resting on the chair. Keep the legs relaxed. Your hands are placed at the sides of your thighs.

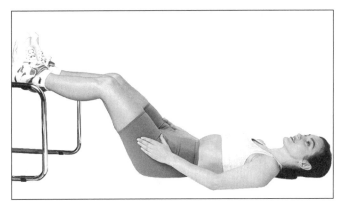

Action

▶ Bring your chin down a fraction as you exhale and lift, sliding the arms up your thighs. Come up on counts 1 and 2, hold on count 3, and return to the start position on count 4.

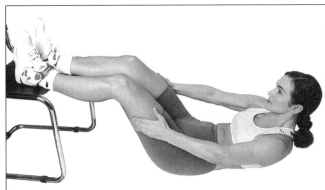

▶ Repeat. Start with 4 reps, and gradually work up to two sets of 8–16 reps.

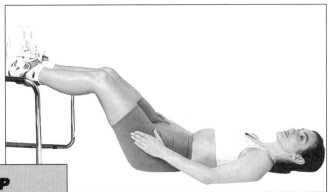

TRAINING TIP

▶ Try not to release too quickly as you return to the start position on count 4. Instead, slowly uncurl your spine down towards the floor.

PLAN FOUR

CRUNCH ON THE BIAS

There are two separate stages to this crunch. Be especially careful to maintain the correct body positioning throughout to ensure maximum benefits and protect your back.

Start

▶ One leg is placed on a pouffe or *very low* chair, the other leg is placed on the floor. Hands are cradling your head. Your body is positioned on a diagonal so that your weight is slightly over to one side – not directly on your side or on your back but somewhere between the two. This is the direction in which you will be moving on the first stage of the crunch.

Action

▶ Exhale as you lift, aiming the underarm area of the top arm towards the hip on the same side. (This is a variation on the standard oblique movement.) Return to the start position and repeat. Start with a low number of repetitions, say 4, increasing the number as you become stronger. When you have completed your repetitions on this side, return to the floor and keep the same leg raised to move on to the second stage of this exercise.

▶ Extend the arm as shown, to act as your lead in this next stage. The other hand is supporting your head. Pull the abdominals in and up, and prepare to exhale.

▶ Exhale as you lift, and reach across the body towards the raised leg. Make sure you keep your lower body firmly in position so that your hips do not move. Return to the floor and repeat. Again, start with 4 reps and build up from there.

▶ Repeat this whole sequence of movements on the other side, making sure you do an equal number of repetitions on each side. You want to aim to get up to two sets of 8–16 reps of both stages of the exercise and on each side.

TRAINING TIP

▶ Position, position, position is everything in this exercise! Keep your lower body stable throughout the exercise. Don't let it swing with you as you move your upper body.

PLAN FOUR

ELEVATED OBLIQUES

Start

▶ Cross your ankles and tuck your knees in towards your chest as far as possible, holding your abdomen flat. Extend one arm out to the side along the floor to act as a stabilizer. This arm will remain on the floor. Cradle your head with the other hand.

TRAINING TIP

▶ Use the arm on the floor to stabilize your body and prevent you from moving your hips.

Action

▶ Lift your shoulder and rib cage then add a twist, aiming the shoulder towards the outstretched arm.

▶ Return to the start position and repeat. Start with 4 reps, and build up to two sets of 8–16 reps.

Just because the legs are relaxed in towards the body, don't forget to keep the abdomen flat throughout.

TOUGH CRUNCH

Start

▶ Have your feet a comfortable distance away from your buttocks. Your arms are outstretched behind your head, hands crossed at the wrists and fingers extended. Keep the arms beside the head to provide support.

Action

▶ Exhale as you lift, holding your abdomen flat. Your arms, head, shoulders and rib cage move in one smooth unit.

▶ Return to the start position and repeat. Start with 4 reps, and gradually build up to two sets of 8–16 reps.

TRAINING TIP

▶ As the name implies, this one is tough. Just come up as far as you can, ensuring the movement is initiated and maintained by the strength of your abs.

PLAN FOUR

DOUBLE REACH

Start

▶ One leg is raised, with the knee bent. Your hands are cradling your head. Pull your abs in and up as you prepare to lift.

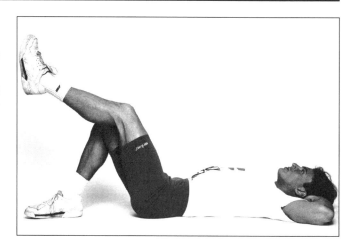

TRAINING TIP

▶ Since your head is not supported during this crunch, remember to bring your chin down slightly, but keep your head in neutral as you lift. Take care to ensure your head maintains its position and does not bob back and forth with the movement.

Action

▶ Exhale, pressing your abdomen down towards your spine and then up towards your rib cage as you lift, extending the raised leg and reaching both arms first up then past the outside of this leg. Remember, the twist comes from your waist, so make sure the opposite shoulder and rib cage are aiming towards the raised leg.

▶ Return to the start position and repeat. Try 4 reps at first, eventually working up to two sets of 8–16 reps.

▶ Repeat to the other side.

CLIMBING CRUNCH

Start

▶ The soles of your feet are placed flat against a wall. Keep your knees away from the centre of your torso, so that the body is nice and long. Your arms are raised in front, with hands in loose fists. Imagine you are holding a rope. Get a good grip on the 'rope', because it is going to help you up. Pull your abs in and up as you prepare to 'climb up'.

Action

▶ Exhale as you climb up the rope, keeping the feet firmly in place. Climb as far as you can on 4 counts, maintaining your head and your pelvic region in neutral. As soon as it becomes difficult to hold your abs in and up, release the rope and return to the floor on a slow count of 4.

▶ Repeat. Start with 4 reps, progressing to two sets of 8–16 reps. With each repetition, you climb up on 4 counts and return to the floor on 4 counts.

Always remember to check your neutral position before commencing the crunch.

TRAINING TIPS

▶ Although you are using the wall for support, try to avoid pressing the feet too hard against it.

▶ Visualization really helps in this exercise. If you can see that rope, we guarantee you'll climb higher.

PLAN FOUR

KILLER CRUNCH

There are four counts to this series of movements. Your upper body will be up off the floor for three of these counts – hence the name 'killer'. The first few times you attempt this exercise you may wish simply to move slowly through each stage to familiarize yourself with the movements before starting to count your repetitions. Each stage needs to be clearly defined. Move cleanly into each position and hold it, rather than letting your body waver up and down.

Remember to maintain your head and pelvis in neutral position and press your abdomen in and up on all phases of the lift.

Start

▶ Start on the floor with hands cradling your head. Check you are in neutral, then come up into a Clean Crunch. Stay up in this crunch.

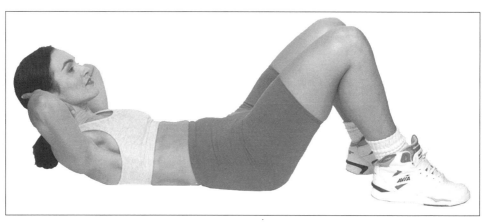

Action

▶ From the top of your Clean Crunch, you are going to increase the range of motion a little by extending your arms forward. Keep your abs in and up.

PLAN FOUR

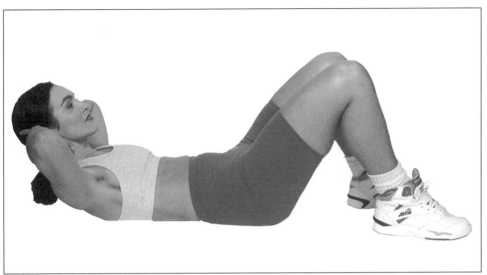

▶ This stage requires the most concentration. Exhale, pressing your abs down once more as you bring the arms back down to your head while remaining up in your Clean Crunch. Do not let your upper body move back to the floor.

TRAINING TIP

▶ As your arms come back down to your head on count 3, resist the inclination to return directly to the floor by pressing your abs down and lifting higher.

▶ Now, return to the floor and take a breather before repeating the exercise – you deserve it! Try 4 reps at first, and slowly progress to two sets of 8–16 reps.

PLAN FOUR

KAREN'S CRUNCH

One of Karen's favourites, this is an extremely challenging exercise. Here, the legs are unsupported, so it is essential that your abs are strong enough to hold the body in position while completing the lift and your legs are towards your torso just enough to avoid overstressing the back.

Start

▶ Both legs are raised and bent towards you – just enough to prevent you from feeling any discomfort in your back. Your legs are going to remain in this position throughout the exercise. Arms are extended above your head, close by your ears, to provide head support.

TRAINING TIP

▶ During your exhalation and lift, the entire spine creates a long 'C' curve, as if both ends of the rectus abdominis muscle are approaching each other. Think of this curve extending from the top of your legs, up through the pubic region and right up to the top of your arms.

Action

▶ The movement is initiated by flattening and then lifting your abdominal wall. Exhale as you gently round the spine. Feel the movement through the whole of your spine as it curls up towards the ceiling to bring your rib cage towards your pelvis. As you lift, your head, arms, shoulders and rib cage move in one smooth unit.

▶ Return to the start position and repeat. Start with just 4 reps, building up to two sets of 8–16 reps.

PLAN FOUR

COUPLE CRUNCH

This Couple Crunch – or 'fun crunch' as some people might call it – is not an essential part of Plan Four. We have introduced it as an extra motivational factor – working out with your partner. You will need a towel for this exercise. Roll up the towel as shown.

Start

 One person kneels on the floor, while the other stands behind them holding the top of the towel. The person who is kneeling takes hold of the other end, grasping them tightly. It is this person who will be doing the work.

Action

▶ The standing partner maintains his/her position, keeping a firm grip on the towel. Meanwhile, the kneeling partner exhales, pulling the abs in and up and really concentrating on curling the spine, using the resistance provided by the standing partner. The kneeling partner should avoid pulling with the arms – it's the abdominals that do the work.

▶ Start with 4 reps and build up from there to a maximum of two sets of 8–16 reps. Remember to swap over positions, so that each of you has a chance to work those abs.

TRAINING TIP
▶ To increase the resistance of the exercise, the standing partner can pull away from the action with the towel.

Now proceed to your cool-down exercises on pages 92–100.

COOLING DOWN

After your workout it is important to stretch out the major muscle groups you have been working in order to minimize any soreness and help prevent injury.

Now that your body temperature is elevated as a result of your workout you can now aim to increase flexibility here. Hold each of the following stretches for a minimum of twenty counts.

COOLING DOWN

1. Neck Stretch

▶ Sitting up tall, place one hand on the opposite side of your head. Let the other arm rest by your side.

▶ Gently lower one ear towards the shoulder, applying gentle pressure with the hand. As you lower the ear, push the shoulder down towards the floor, away from the head. Hold, then release.

▶ Repeat to the other side.

2. Seated Round Over

▶ Sit up tall and raise your arms above your head, interlocking the fingers. Keep the shoulders relaxed and down.

▶ Maintaining that tall feeling, slowly round your back, pulling your abs in and up. Feel the stretch in your back. Hold, then lift back up to the start position.

Remember to hold each stretch for at least 20 counts.

COOLING DOWN

3. Complete Back Stretch

COOLING DOWN

► Lying on your back, clasp your hands under your knees and bring the knees towards your chest.

► In one smooth action, exhale while lifting your head and shoulders towards the knees. Feel the stretch in your back. Hold, then release.

COOLING DOWN

4. Leg Cross-over

▶ Lie with legs extended and your body relaxed. Lift one knee in towards your chest and place the opposite hand on the outside of the leg, just above the knee.

▶ Use your hand to bring the leg across your body. At first, keep both shoulders and as much of your back on the floor as is possible and feel the stretch at the hip. Then allow the knee to go further to extend the stretch into your lower back. Hold, then release.

▶ Repeat with the other leg.

COOLING DOWN

5. Forward Lunge

▶ Support yourself on one knee as shown. Your hands are in line with your front foot. Keep your chest lifted, your upper back flat, with shoulders back and down. Your neck is in neutral, following its natural curve. Take care not to let the head drop forward.

▶ Keeping your torso lifted, slowly lunge forward onto your front leg, ensuring the knee remains above the ankle. Feel the stretch in the front thigh of the back leg. Hold, then release.

▶ Repeat with the other leg.

9 7

COOLING DOWN

6. C-Curve

In this exercise you are going to move the shoulder and hip towards each other so that the spine makes a C-curve to the side. This lengthens the muscles responsible for bending the body sideways.

▶ Position yourself on all fours. Your knees are in line with your hips, elbows under your shoulders, hands under your elbows. Your back is flat and your head in neutral.

▶ Bring your head towards one shoulder and aim the shoulder towards the hip on that side. At the same time bring the hip to the side as if to meet the shoulder. Hold, then release.

▶ Repeat to the other side.

7. Side Stretch

▶ Stand tall with feet a little wider than hip-width apart, knees slightly bent. Place one hand on your thigh and reach up with the other arm. Keep your spine and neck in neutral and your shoulders back and down.

▶ Slowly reach over to the side, feeling the stretch in your waist. Hold, then release.

Remember to hold each stretch for at least 20 counts.

▶ Repeat to the other side.

COOLING DOWN

8. Standing Round Over

▶ Bend your knees, leaning slightly forward from the hips. Place your hands on the front of your thighs. Keep your back straight and your torso lifted.

▶ Maintaining that lift, slowly round your back, tucking your abdomen in. Feel the stretch in your back. Hold, then release.

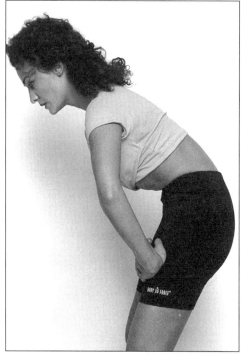

You are now ready to move on to your back strengthening exercises. Turn to page 103.

CHAPTER 4

Back Problems and Solutions

THE PROBLEM

Anyone who has ever suffered from back pain knows just how debilitating this can be. As we have seen in Chapter 1, evidence suggests that many common back problems may be related to poor abdominal strength. Nowadays, most of us spend our time either sitting with shoulders slumped forward, or standing with our weight over to one side of the body, both of which, over time, can overstress the back.

Over a number of years these bad posture habits can lead to a deterioration in the structures of the back, greatly reducing our mobility and seriously affecting our ability to perform everyday physical tasks. When the back is in a weak state, the application of a sudden force – for instance reaching up or lifting an object off the ground – can cause chronic pain and/or injury. Often this pain is not just felt in the back, but it can also affect other areas of the body. So what's the reason for this?

The spinal column is made up of a series of vertebrae (see page 14). These are the bony sections of the spine. In between each vertebra is a small spongy disc, the nucleus of which contains viscous fluid. It is these discs that form the soft tissue of the spine, enabling the muscles to move the spine in a variety of movements such as rotating the torso, bending forward or backward, allowing for a certain amount of resiliency and impact without injuring the structures of the back.

However, when we perform any kind of spinal movement, in particular arching or rounding the back, we change the pressure on these discs. Poor posture and fast, jerky movements can render this pressure uneven. Over a prolonged period of time the constant application of uneven pressure will eventually cause these spongy discs to protrude. In severe cases this can result in a ruptured disc and a subsequent loss of fluid from the disc, which substantially decreases the flexibility in that area. The protrusion of the discs can also put pressure on the major nerve stems that run along the

spinal column. This not only causes a great deal of pain and discomfort in the back, but it can also affect neurological function in other parts of the body such as the shoulders and the backs of the legs. Sciatica is a prime example of what can occur when constant pressure is placed on a nerve.

This is why we need to take care when undertaking any exercises, but in particular those for the back.

THE SOLUTION

This crunch programme, combined with some simple back strengthening and stretching exercises, can significantly reduce your likelihood of suffering low-back problems.

The muscles of the back work in opposition to the abdominals, and their muscular structures are quite different. Unlike the abdominals, the back muscles vary considerably in length. Some are quite long, extending the full length of the back, while others are extremely short, running from one verterbra to another. Having these short muscles means that the back is naturally strong yet relatively inflexible. This is one of the reasons why we need to do specific stretching exercises for the back.

When we work the muscles at the front of the body, we also involve the muscles at the back. Therefore, when we strengthen the abdomen and waist area, as in this crunch programme, it is important to include some back strengthening as well as stretching exercises at the end of our workout to prevent an imbalance of strength and flexibility between the abdominal and back muscles.

In this section you will find a few, very simple back strengthening exercises followed by some cool-down stretches. These exercises will also lengthen the abdominal muscles, enhancing the effectiveness of your preceding crunch programme.

In order to achieve maximum benefits in terms of strength and flexibility these exercises should always be performed slowly and deliberately to allow the use of muscle force throughout your full range of motion. Doing them in a smooth, controlled fashion ensures that most of the muscle fibres in the spinal area are recruited, providing optimum training benefits while ensuring that the spine and discs are well supported. Fast, jerky movements can put you at risk of low-back injury and also greatly decrease the effectiveness of the exercises.

Anyone who has an existing back problem should consult a doctor or physiotherapist to assess their individual needs before undertaking any exercise programme.

BACK STRENGTHENING

It is not essential to do all these exercises after your crunch workout. You may want to just start with the first three, but we do recommend you always include the Cat Curl in your programme. This is an extremely safe exercise, good for both stretching and strengthening and is therefore especially beneficial for anyone suffering from a tight or inflexible back. An effective back strengthening routine could therefore include the Cat Curl plus any two additional exercises from this section. Always finish with the back cool-down stretches on pages 109–112.

> *Remember, if you feel any discomfort or pain during any of these exercises, stop immediately and avoid that particular exercise until your strength and control increases.*

THE CRUNCH

CAT CURL

This can be a stretch or a strengthening exercise, depending on how it is performed. Here, we are using the strengthening element.

Start

▶ Start on hands and knees in the all fours position. Place your elbows under your shoulders and your hands under your elbows. Your knees are hip-width apart and directly under your hips. Your abdominals are lifted in and up. Keep your back flat and your head in line with your spine.

Action

▶ You are going to slowly round your spine up towards the ceiling as far as you can. Pull your abs in and up to initiate the movement, then follow through with a full rounding. Hold for a count of 10, increasing the count as your body becomes stronger.

▶ Now, you are going to do the opposite of the above. *Without* using momentum, slowly move your spine into a concave position, pushing your belly button towards the floor. Your neck and buttocks are raised towards the ceiling as far they can *comfortably* go. *This is not a movement you want to force.* At first, hold for a count of 4, then release. As your back becomes stronger you will be able to hold this position for longer.

THE CRUNCH

OPPOSITE ARM AND LEG REACH

Start

▶ Lie face down with arms outstretched above your head. Your abdomen is lifted, but make sure both hip bones remain on the floor. You are going to reach the opposite arm and leg away from each other, following through with a small lift. If you wish, you can turn your head towards the arm you will be reaching, but keep your neck relaxed.

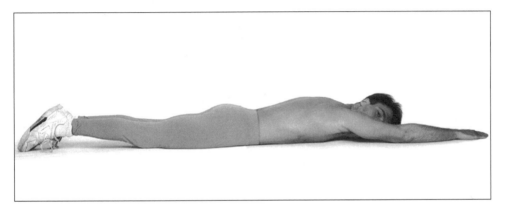

Action

▶ Keeping your abdomen in and up, reach the opposite arm away from the leg. As you reach, the arm and leg will eventually come off the floor. As the leg comes off the floor, make sure you keep the hips down.

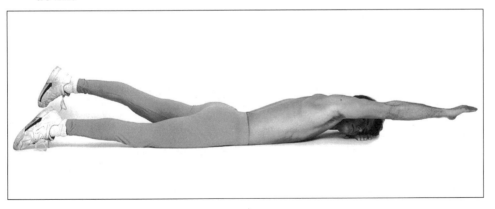

▶ Return the arm and leg to the floor and repeat. Start with 8–10 reps, adding another set as soon as this becomes easy.

▶ Repeat with the other arm and leg.

THE CRUNCH

BACK EXTENSION

Start

► Lie face down with hands at the back of your head, fingers open. Make sure your legs are together and firmly on the floor.

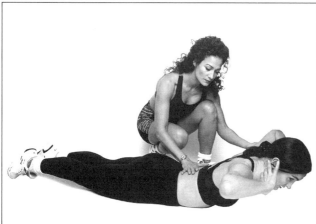

Action

► The action here is the opposite to a Clean Crunch. Keep the movement *slow and controlled*. Slowly raise your upper body off the floor. Think of lengthening your body through the top of your head, rather than aiming for height. Keep your head in neutral and your hips firmly on the floor.

► Return to the start position and repeat. As this exercise is quite difficult, start with 4 reps, increasing the number as you become stronger. If you tire after your first or second attempt or find your upper body does not appear to be lifting away from the floor, discontinue the exercise and return to it after your next crunch workout.

Note: *It is not necessary to have a partner to help you complete this exercise. We have included a trainer in this photograph to indicate the direction and height of the lift. Note that the trainer's hand is placed on the low-back region to ensure that the upper body is not lifted too high.*

ALL FOURS STABILIZER

As well as strengthening the back, this exercise has the added benefit of helping to improve balance.

Start

▶ Start in the all fours position, with hands, elbows and shoulders aligned. Your knees are under your hips, and your back is flat.

Action

▶ Slowly extend the opposite arm and leg together in a smooth, controlled fashion. Keep the leg and arm level with your head and hips, rather than aiming them upward. You are fighting against gravity to hold that flat position from the top of your head right down to the heel of the raised foot. In order to hold your back flat you will need to divide your weight evenly between the supporting hand and leg. Once you have achieved the correct position, hold for a count of 4, then release.

▶ Return the arm and leg to the floor and repeat as many times as is comfortable. Gradually build up to 8 reps, holding each for a count of 4.

▶ Repeat with the other arm and leg, ensuring you do an equal number of repetitions on each side.

Note the location of the trainer's hands in the photographs. This is to indicate how the tightening of the abdominals holds the hips and lower back firmly in place to avoid a swayback (exaggerated arch) position.

THE CRUNCH

THE CRUNCH

STRAIGHTEN OUT

Start

▶ Kneel in the all fours position, this time resting your weight on your forearms. Your heels are raised so that you are up on the balls of your feet. Your back is straight and your neck maintains its natural curve.

Action

▶ Keeping your back flat and your weight evenly distributed between both forearms, slowly straighten your legs. Make sure your abs are pulled in and up to help you hold the position. Hold for a count of 4, maintaining your neck in neutral, then slowly release the knees down to the floor.

▶ Repeat as many times as you can, working up to 8 reps and holding each for for a count of four.

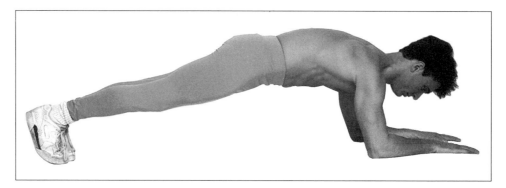

Let's turn to the next page for the back cool-down exercises.

BACK COOL-DOWN

1. Complete Back Stretch

It is natural to feel a certain amount of pressure in your back when you first start to perform back strengthening exercises, but this feeling will gradually diminish as you become stronger. This stretch will help relieve some of that initial pressure.

▶ Lie with your knees towards your chest, hands clasped under your knees.

▶ Slowly raise your head and shoulders towards your knees. Hold for a slow count of 8 or until you feel a relief of pressure.

▶ Repeat this stretch at least 3 or 4 times.

THE CRUNCH

THE CRUNCH

2. Leg Cross-over

Here, we are concentrating on lengthening the back.

▶ Lie flat with your body relaxed. Lift one knee in towards your chest and place the opposite hand on the outside of the leg, just above the knee.

▶ Keeping both shoulders on the floor, bring the leg across the body and feel the stretch in your mid- and low-back. Hold for a minimum of 20 counts, then release.

▶ Repeat with the other leg.

THE CRUNCH

3. Neck Stretch

During your crunch programme you will find the neck muscles tend to fatigue quite easily, especially when you first start. This stretch will help avoid any soreness.

▶ Sit up tall with one hand placed on the opposite side of the head as shown.

▶ Gently pull the head to one side while pushing the shoulder on the same side down towards the floor, away from the head. Hold for a count of 8.

▶ Repeat on the other side, then repeat again on both sides, each time holding for a count of 8.

111

THE CRUNCH

4. Front Shoulder Stretch

During most of your crunches your arms are either held behind your head or extended at the sides of your head. This means your arms are having to constantly pull against gravity, entailing a great deal of work for the shoulder muscles. Let's finish this section with a shoulder stretch.

▶ Sit upright with hands clasped behind your back and feel the stretch in your shoulders.

▶ To increase this stretch, run your hands back along the floor until you feel some mild tension in your shoulders. Hold this position until you begin to feel this tension ease, then try to run your hands back a little further, again until you feel some mild tension. Hold for a count of 20, then release.

▶ If your shoulders still feel tight, repeat this stretch.

Doesn't that feel good? You've been working well and should now be reaping the rewards. Remember, your consistency will pay off in the end when you discover a stronger body and a flatter stomach.

CHAPTER 5

Keep on Crunching

Now that you have mastered the Crunch Challenge and are confident with the exercises in each plan, you can step up the pace and further personalize your programme by adding more variety. You can interchange the crunch gameplans as you wish, or you may prefer to select a few of your favourite exercises and complete them in succession. Even if you have already achieved the shape and tone you want, you will still need to work out three times a week to keep the muscles strong.

However, if you perform the same exercises in the same fashion, after a period of time you can hit a plateau where the results of your workout stabilize and your rate of progress slows down. The best way of ensuring ongoing progress is to 'shock' the muscles regularly. The way you do this is to vary the way you perform an exercise, for example by

▶ changing the count
▶ increasing the range of motion for an extra count
▶ accentuating the movement on the upward phase
▶ accentuating the movement on the downward phase

Each of the above suggestions changes the way you stimulate your muscles. This prevents you from reaching that plateau, enabling you to create a constant challenge.

On the following pages you will find twelve variations on a selection of crunches taken from Plans One to Four. It may be that your favourite exercise is not included here. Be creative and choose any of the counts from the examples given and incorporate these into some of the other crunches to customize your programme further.

Note that in these variations we have not included multi-phased exercises such as the Mummy Crunch. The reason for this is that if an exercise already has several phases and you then add a complex count

THE CRUNCH

variation, you may find it difficult to concentrate on the most important aspect of your workout – holding your abdomen flat throughout your crunches.

Now that you have reached this advanced stage, remember to use your abdominal strength and control in your posture when standing, sitting, walking – in fact in all your everyday activities. This is the secret of maintaining that flat stomach. Welcome to the new you.

Keep on crunching!

Remember, when customizing your own programme you should still always begin with the warm-up and finish with the cool-down. Incorporate some back strengthening into your programme and follow with the back cool-down stretches. Stretching will help prevent stiffness, preserve or increase your range of motion and help you to perform everyday physical tasks with greater ease.

VARIATIONS

BREATHING CRUNCH

▶ Have your hands on your abdomen to ensure you are using your breathing to flatten your abs as you lift your upper body.

▶ Come up on counts 1…2. Breathe out and try to flatten your abdomen further 3…4…5. Return to the floor 6…7…8.

▶ Repeat as many times as you can, eventually working up to two sets of 8–16 reps.

CLEAN CRUNCH

▶ Come up quickly with the accent on count 1. Slowly return to the floor 2…3…4.

▶ Repeat as many times as you can, gradually working up to two sets of 8–16 reps.

▶ A further variation would be to reverse the accent so that you come up slowly on counts 1…2…3 and return to the floor on count 4.

THE CRUNCH

THE CRUNCH

OBLIQUE CRUNCH

▶ Twist, bringing shoulder towards opposite knee, on counts 1…2…3. Return to the floor on count 4. Repeat to the other side.

▶ Repeat as many times as you can, at first twisting to alternate sides. Then, aim to build up your number of repetitions on one side before twisting to the other side. This will step up the challenge even further. Gradually work up to two sets of 8–16 reps on each side.

THIGH SLIDE

▶ Come up slowly, sliding hands towards knees as shown. As you reach the full range of motion at the top of your crunch, place hands on the sides of legs and hold your torso up with your arms. Breathe out, pressing abs further down and then up and hold for 8 counts. Slowly roll back down to the floor.

▶ Repeat 4–8 times. As your strength increases, hold the count for longer. Really feel your abs flattening as you hold.

THE CRUNCH

BUTTERFLY CRUNCH

This variation increases the challenge yet, because the hip flexors are relaxed in this crunch, the position is easy to maintain.

► Come up slowly on counts 1…2. Roll down 3…4. Come right up 5. 6. 7. 8, lifting higher on each count. Stay up and repeat the sequence. The object here is not to return to the floor after count 8, but to lift up further as you begin count 1 again.

► Repeat as many times as you can, aiming to build up to two sets of 8–16 reps. At first you may wish to return to the floor for a breather after each repetition. Once you have achieved sufficient strength you can make the variation more challenging by completing your repetitions without rolling all the way back down to the floor.

SEATED REVERSE CRUNCH

► Slowly curl spine backward on counts 1…2…3…4…5. Come up again 6…7…8.

► Repeat as many times as you can, rounding your back and keeping your abs lifted in and up. Work up to two sets of 8–16 reps. Make sure you round your back rather than bending from the top of the thighs.

THE CRUNCH

AIR BIKE

In this variation you are going to perform two twists to each side in turn, bringing the shoulder and opposite knee towards each other. Keep the movements slow and controlled.

▶ Twist up on count 1, twist torso higher on count 2. Repeat to the other side.

▶ Repeat the 'double twist' 8–16 times to each side in turn, without returning to the floor in between repetitions.

FULL EXTENSION

▶ Lift up, holding your abs flat as you extend both arms and legs towards the ceiling. Stay up and hold for 4 counts. Return to the floor, bending your knees towards your torso and bringing the arms down.

▶ Repeat 8–16 times.

BOXER CRUNCH

▶ Your heels are resting on a chair to maintain your pelvis in neutral. Lift up on counts 1...2. Hold in pec press 3...4. Return to the floor 5...6...7...8.

▶ Repeat 8–16 times.

CRUNCH ON THE BIAS

In this variation we are using only the first phase of this crunch. Your body is positioned on a diagonal with feet supported on a low chair or pouffe. The underarm area of the top arm is going to approach the hip on the same side.

▶ Lift up slowly on counts 1...2. Lower torso 3...4. Lift up again 5...6. Lower torso 7...8. Now come right up on 1. 2. 3. 4. 5. 6. 7. 8, lifting torso higher on each count. Stay up and repeat the sequence.

▶ Repeat 4–8 times, then repeat on the other side. Once you are strong enough you can aim to complete your repetitions without rolling all the way back down to the floor for a breather.

THE CRUNCH

119

THE CRUNCH

CLIMBING CRUNCH

▶ With feet placed against a wall, climb up on 8 counts. Slowly return to the floor on 8 counts.

▶ Repeat 4–8 times, climbing up higher on each repetition.

KILLER CRUNCH

▶ Come up on counts 1…2…3…4. Reach arms forward 5…6…7…8. Maintaining your lift, bring arms back to your head 1…2…3…4. Slowly return to the floor 5…6…7…8.

▶ Repeat 4–8 times.

The Crunch Training Log

Keeping a record of your progress can be extremely valuable, especially when first starting out on your crunch programme. A common practice in the field of fitness, it is widely recognized that by keeping track of your goals you are more likely to be consistent in achieving them. Make several copies of the blank log on page 122 so that you can continue to monitor your progress whichever plan you are following or whichever combination of exercises you may choose when customizing your own programme. A real motivator would be to stick up a copy of the log in a highly visible place. Don't forget to note any changes you have made to your eating habits and any other exercise or activity you have undertaken that week.

Remember to chart your results immediately after your workout, since it is easy to forget later how much you have accomplished.

The Crunch Training Log

PLAN ONE STARTING OUT	Week starting: No. of sets/reps	Week starting: No. of sets/reps
FINDING NEUTRAL		
BREATHING TECHNIQUE		
BREATHING CRUNCH		
CLEAN CRUNCH		
OBLIQUE CRUNCH		
REACH OUT		
REACH OUT AND FLEX		
GO FOR IT		
CROSS-OVER CRUNCH		
COMPLETED BACK STRENGTHENING Y/N		
NO. OF TIMES CRUNCH PROGRAMME COMPLETED PER WEEK		
NOTES (eating/other activity)		

	Week starting:							Week starting:						
	No. of sets/reps							No. of sets/reps						
COMPLETED BACK STRENGTHENING Y/N														
NO. OF TIMES CRUNCH PROGRAMME COMPLETED PER WEEK														
NOTES (eating/other activity)														